BOWERY
BLUES

BOWERY BLUES

A Tribute to Dorothy Day

Jack Cook

OTHER BOOKS BY JACK COOK:

Rags of Time: A Season in Prison 1972

The Face of Falsehood 1986

Library of Congress #:   2001117871

ISBN #:   Softcover   0-7388-6362-9

This book was printed in the United States of America.

To order additional copies of this book, contact:
Xlibris Corporation
1-888-7-XLIBRIS
www.Xlibris.com
Orders@Xlibris.com

CONTENTS

INTRODUCTION

I have always thought of myself as a half-assed poet and passable prose writer. So I was somewhat shocked (but secretly quite pleased) when in the fall of 1968, while being driven by Dorothy Day from the East First Street House of Hospitality to the printers in the Bronx, to put the latest issue of the Catholic Worker to bed, she instructed me (she did not encourage or suggest) to get my pieces (the bulk of what is here) collected into a book. I'm a little late in getting to it. First, prison, then the rest of my life intervened. Each decade since has been marked by dejection slips from publishers large and small, left, center, and main. Not topical now, they said, or Write something new, or You're not a name that will sell.

My favorite epigraph on the wall of the Chrystie Street office was "'Success is not the name of God' Leon Bloy."

So I take the opportunity offered by this new technology, which I neither understand or can use, in order to comply with Dorothy's directions and to lift that weight from my psyche. Besides, I never kept a journal or a diary during my years at the Worker, so these early works are the only record I have, apart from a scarred memory. I include here all the later pieces of mine the Worker published over the years, the last being from 1997, as well as the tribute to her from the Preface to my *Rags of Time: A Season in Prison* (Beacon, 1972); also, the unpublished "Open Letter To The Catholic Worker" of 1998, and two unpublished poems, one on Missouri Marie's death, the other a response to Cardinal O'Connor's letter "Dorothy Day's Sainthood Cause Begins," (St. Patrick's Day, 2000) which concludes this work.

I use the word "tribute" not in its slipshod sense, as the Fowler brothers would have it, that is to do the work of "a proof" as in 'a tribute of my esteem'; but in its figurative sense, 'a contribution, especially a thing done, said, given as a mark of respect.' Each of these pieces was composed as a gift to Dorothy. It was for all of us always Dorothy's paper from whence thundered forth her voice. We could only add ours to hers. The earliest pieces, dating back to the fall of 1966, when all the pots were boiling, especially the Chrystie and 36 East First Street pieces, were written on a Tuesday night for a Wednesday deadline, when the need for an article out-weighed all other needs that had to be met. We were a need-based operation then; the term "faith-based" had not yet been coined.

If Dorothy appears but seldom in these pages, that is how it was meant to be. It was understood that I was not there to do P.R. work, but to document the work we were doing, other workers, and the issues: to tell stories and describe people who incarnated our ideas and ideals—ultimately Dorothy's vision.

ACKNOWLEDGMENTS

I cannot hope to acknowledge all those whose voices and faces generated these pieces. They were vital and present to me then; may they now once again step forth from the faded page. I must, however, acknowledge the intensely critical, first-rate mind of Martin Corbin, my first editor, whose pen gleaned my style, whose confidence gave me leeway. I must also acknowledge Jane Sammon, Associate Editor of the CW, for her assistance in getting old copies of the Worker reproduced by assuring my local Kinkos that there was no copyright problem , the CW being uncopyrighted. I am grateful, also, to Tara Murtha, Publishing Associate of Xlibris, for her assistance was professional, her guidance kind and considerate. Finally, I am indebted to my daughter Cynthia (Cinta) for prepar-ing a manuscript in a fashion beyond my abilities, that is on disk.

O for a voice like thunder, and a tongue
To drown the throat of war: When the senses
Are shaken, and the soul is driven to madness,
Who can stand? When the souls of the oppressed
Fight in the troubled air that rages, who can stand?
When the whirlwind of fury comes from the
Throne of God, when the frowns of his countenance
Drive the nations together, who can stand?
When Sin claps his broad wings over the battle,
And sails rejoicing in the flood of Death;
When souls are torn to everlasting fire,
And fiends of Hell rejoice upon the slain,
O who can stand? O who hath caused this?
O who can answer at the throne of God?
The Kings and Nobles of the Land have done it!
Hear it not, Heaven, thy Ministers have done it!

William Blake
"Prologue, intended for a Dramatic Piece of King Edward the Fourth"

A TRIBUTE TO DOROTHY DAY

From *Rags of Time* by Jack Cook

Having severed my connection with Selective Service while an instructor in English at Hobart and William Smith Colleges, Geneva, New York, in the spring of 1966, thereafter to join the peace movement as an editor of The Catholic Worker, a pacifist-anarchist monthly in New York City, I was indicted, tried, and convicted for Refusal To Be Induced into the Armed Forces of the United States and sentenced to three years in prison on 4 January 1969 out of the Southern District Court, Foley Square, New York City, by Judge Metzner. After spending a week or so in the West Street Federal Detention Center in Manhattan, I was bussed, handcuffed to another prisoner, together with twenty-five other prisoners to Lewisburg Federal Penitentiary in Lewisburg, Pennsylvania. From there, after two weeks of the administration's and the inmate's orientation to prison life, I was sent to Allenwood Federal Prison Camp, located some fifteen miles away, an adjunct of the larger walled-in Lewisburg prison.

For me there was a beginning when I first heard Dorothy Day of *The Catholic Worker* at one of the Friday night meetings in the old Chrystie Street House of Hospitality on the Bowery, a place I soon came to love and hated to leave two years later when the community moved up to East First Street. She seemed weary. At that time she was sixty-eight and she spoke as if the end were near.

(At seventy-two she still seems weary. But I know now her lurking gaiety. And she still speaks as if the end were near. But the slightest chore will put it off.) Yet in that summer of 1966, speaking and being heard as one with little time left, she thought it imperative to talk about Anarchy.

She turned her mind and, as it were, her face toward the State; and, had it been there in that shabby room instead of us, it would have withered under that stare. No abstract ideology was forthcoming. She needed no mask to attend the Revolutionary Ball. Instead there were the anecdotes of governmental and corporate injustice she had seen over five decades and the stories of what this one and that one, names and nicknames, had done to alleviate the state-imposed pain. Direct, personal action; make the need of the oppressed your need; do for them, with them, what it would be impossible for them to do alone. No structure, no hierarchy, no formulated program; just people helping other people.

She reminded me of Emma Goldman, as my friend Dick Drinnon in his definitive biography presented her to his readers. Physically, she was as imposing as her predecessor; the same power, the same presence. And, like Emma, she offered the anarchism of Kropotkin, combined, though, not with the individualism of Ibsen, but with the mysticism and radical Christianity of Dostoevsky and Tolstoy.

Both women looked to a destructured, unauthoritarian society of equal individuals. "The individual is the heart of society," Emma said and Dorothy would certainly agree. Both envisioned "small organic organizations in free-cooperation with each other," as Dick Drinnon phrased it. But Dorothy was standing in, and could look back at, her dream and that of Peter Maurin (the co-founder of *The Catholic Worker*): a community within the shell of a larger community: the House of Hospitality that had, together with her newspaper, continued to survive, when other radical movements originating in the Thirties were but a memory or a travesty.

Both saw through, and the glance was indeed intrepid, the myths of the state, the corrosive manipulation of peoples, the repression and domination. Both looked upon liberal solutions, not conservatism's frantic gestures, as being the greater evil. Both turned indignant maternal glances on the budget of the Federal government that spends millions upon defense, so little on human needs. Both knew that real freedom must begin with personal freedom, internalized revolution, absolute conversion. Both incarnated Female Emancipation, Women's Liberation.

Both could look back, with bitterness, at a long series of lost causes, dashed hopes, disillusionment, and folly. For Emma there were Berkman jailed, a revolution caricatured, Sacco and Vanzetti, Berkman's suicide, the bloody executions, the defeat in Spain, repeated jailings, and the image of a "national bugaboo." For Dorothy there were the loss of old friends turned off by her pacifism during the Spanish Civil War, others turned liberal; the despair of the World War II period, when her stance further alienated her from leftists and her countrymen; the loss of working class support, never to reappear even as the working class never quite reappeared after the war; constant misunderstandings and ridicule, publication debts, hassles with city government over housing regulations (she was once declared a slum landlord by a city judge) and with Federal government over nonpayment of taxes, repeated jailings, and the innumerable personal tragedies of the constantly growing, constantly dying community for which she was responsible.

Just as during a wet heavy snow, huge pine trees, their dark branches burdened with weight, take on increased stature and greater depth (a sculpture shadowed within, white without), even as the whole aspiring growth languishes—so did these two impassioned defenders of Folly and personal freedom carry into old age the weight of loss and long suffering.

Dorothy, perhaps even more than A.J. Muste and much before Martin Luther King, introduced into the American radical scene militant nonviolent direct action as a tactic with which to confront need and oppression. It was a weapon forged for her out of union struggles of the Twenties and Thirties, the Depression as it hit the Bowery, combined with the fearlessness of the slapped, perhaps, but not overcome radical Christian, and the teachings of Gandhi. Draft card burning, when that was declared a felony, began at the *Worker*. It was a Catholic Worker, Roger La Porte, whose immolation at the United Nations in 1966 threw New York City into its first (officially unexplained) blackout, and paralleled for us the sacrifice of the Buddhist monks of Saigon.

The face of Dorothy Day. The face of one who had descended over half a century ago to the very root of being, and, finding it, stayed—unlike so many honored others. The face of one so rooted in the core of the American and the radical experience, so close to the struggling men at the bottom, that through devotion and endurance, gentleness and solidarity, the heaping up of small things—bread and soup lines, rooms for the homeless, new old clothes, words of union, peace and brotherhood—something high and great took form, bending around obstacles at the root ("When we need money, we pray for it"), and grew, imperceptibly, steadily, unhindered, and undeceived by the outward changes in the American scene. Something high and great, rooted in the squalor of the Lower East Side but penetrating into the very heavens. As the sole tree in the yard of Lewisburg prison absorbs all the dreams of every hung-up prisoner, his mind shattered on the street, as it yields to each prisoner's hopes as the seasons change and naked limbs are clothed in green; so did her compassion absorb the pain of men and women, borne by the time; so did her acceptance of this man's hunger, that woman's homelessness, make their needs her needs; so, too, was her yielding to the castoffs of a city empty of concern, of a government apathetic toward its own victims.

In that shabby soup kitchen on Chrystie Street, I saw flourishing the ideas closest to me—Anarchy, pacifism, radical Christianity. There, alive in the eyes of Dorothy Day, was "The Cretan Glance," as Kazantzakis wrote of it in his last work, *Report to Greco:*

I gazed at the bullfights painted on the walls: the woman's agility and grace, the man's unerring strength, how they played with the frenzied bull, confronting him with intrepid glances. They did not kill him out of love in order to unite with him, as in oriental religions, or because they were overcome with fear and dared not look at him. Instead, they played with him, obstinately, respectfully, without hate. Perhaps even with gratitude. For this sacred battle with the bull whetted the Cretan's strength, cultivated his bodily agility and grace, the fiery yet coolheaded precision of movement, the discipline of will, the valor—so difficult to acquire—to measure his strength against the beast's fearful power without being overcome by panic. Thus the Cretans transubstantiated horror, turning it into an exalted game in which man's virtue, in direct contact with mindless omnipotence, received stimulation and conquered—conquered without annihilating the bull, because it considered him not an enemy but a fellow worker. Without him, the body would not have become so flexible and strong, the soul is so valiant.

Surely a person needs great training of both body and soul if he is to have the endurance to view the beast and play such a dangerous game. But once he is trained and acquires the feel of the game, every one of his movements becomes simple, certain, and leisurely; he looks upon fear with intrepidity.

As I regarded the battle depicted on the walls, the age-old battle between man and bull (whom today we term God), I said to myself, Such was the Cretan Glance.

Such are Dorothy's agility and grace, her unnerving strength, after seven decades on this earth, that her movement of fellow workers, after thirty-eight years on the Lower East Side, still flourishes, still serves, still attracts the gentle faces, torn psyches, the souls hurting from a love they cannot handle; so they ladle soup instead for the uneasy faces, give out clean clothes for rags, and soothe for a time their own and another's torn psyche with love in a hectic home.

I followed my kind to the Bowery. Not the young peace people only, nor the draft resisters (though I was one of them), nor the liberal well-wishers (I was partly that, too); but I followed the Bowery men, my kind: the lost, jobless, sick and lonely, empty and roleless men of the insane Sixties, Fifties, Forties, and Thirties. The children of the Depression; the babies of the Bomb. Men in whom not even the memory of the recollection of the dream of what America might have been—not even *that* survived.

I went to *The Catholic Worker* because it was necessary for me to begin at the beginning. The Bowery is an end. The last ditch. The Gutter of Gutters for hopeless men this whole land wide; yet it is a beginning, too. Where else but at the bottom, after all? When everyone else seemed devoted to making a living, deliberate distraction in spite of the abyss, it was necessary to go where that kind of life had stopped; it was necessary in order to find out what living was all about.

At the beginning, then: Poverty—make it voluntary, yet conniving, a hustle; Community—color it chaotic, demanding, devastating, lonely; Service—label it haughty when not impatient, sometimes disturbing, poignant; Squalor—bedbugs, lice, tedium, druggies, curse the idlers, "sit down" for hours upon hours, get arrested, and arrested; Anarchy—no law from above, Dorothy, not yours, not the churches', not the State's; Unionism—the gentleshrewd Chavez; Propaganda of the Word, Anarchy of the Deed—articles written in haste before deadlines (Dorothy's need) when that overshadowed every other need, speeches, teach-ins, picketing, and marches; Marriage—a union celebrated in the soup kitchen one week before my imprisonment; Celebration—making love in a sleeping bag on a tenement rooftop, drinking with Bowery men, men soon to become Bowery men, with friends; Death—walk with it, talk with it, sleep with it, feed it, clothe it, look at it in the mirror, at the morgue identify it, watch it play around garbage cans, sleep in hallways, shatter into a thousand glittering bloodstained pieces of glass, watch it put Bowery men in Paddy Wagons; Resistance—"I am proud to plead guilty to this charge. To hell with the arrogance of the State!"; Need—for endurance, for flesh to touch flesh, spirit, spirit; for knowledge to make connections, to push a truth through the darkness; to withdraw, at times, from understanding as from "the gulfs their slimed foundations bared"—to be and to be not.

JIM WILSON GETS
THREE YEARS

DECEMBER 1966

Only partially awake, yet fully enraged at the events which were to take place this day (December 9), I descended the stairs of the building on Kenmare Street, where most of the Workers live, and knocked at the door of one of the women's apartments in order to assure myself that I had a ride to Newark, New Jersey, where Jim Wilson, my friend and fellow Catholic Worker, was to be sentenced for committing, as he said in his statement to the court, "this crime: I refuse to kill."

The door opened upon Dorothy and Pat Rusk, both preparing to go to Mass before setting off. Their mood, in utter contrast to mine, was one of joy and gaiety. Miss Day spoke eagerly of the importance and power of Mass, of Jim's act as a form of martyrdom; she spoke, too, of how strongly she felt about Jim, whose absolutist position, unencumbered by lawyers and compromise, stark in its Christianity, was truly that of the Catholic Worker. Mass seemed, however, uppermost in their minds at the moment; rage, unfortunately, being uppermost in mine, I did not ask if I might join them.

The ride from dreary New York to dismal Newark was uneventful, yet fraught with anxiety and tension. Arriving in plenty of time, Dorothy invited Pat and me to breakfast in a restaurant near the Federal Court Building. A joyful breakfast, in her words. But, again, I could not meet that occasion. To be sure, I remembered the joy with which the early Christians are reported to have met their deaths; the perennial Christian paradox: one must die in order to live: that such a death, being in fact an affirmation of life itself as well as the doorstep to a new life, was to be greeted joyfully not mournfully. But I knew Jim Wilson and his wife Raona; we had worked together, talked anxiously about the problems we confronted at the Worker, with the government, in our time. I shared the anxiety and tension which preceded the then unknown date of sentencing; shared, too, their relief when that date was finally made known to them; and, in dread and hope, awaited the passing of sentence.

It was long in coming. We had time to grow accustomed to the pretentious décor of the courtroom; the buzzing tête-à-têtes of lawyers and defendants in the seats around us, oblivious to the drama going on in front of the judge; accustomed to the harsh officiousness of the courtroom detectives, who would not tolerate the babies crying; we grew accustomed, also, to the unvarying formulae—the monotonous repetitions-of Judge Shaw who, in addressing each defendant, addressed him in exactly the same words, informing him of his unparalleled rights and privileges, particular, of course, to the present situation.

Finally, after all the arraignments, after all the dull procedure, the time of Jim's sentencing approached. A Jehovah's Witness, who had pled guilty, as Jim did, to refusing to be inducted, was to be sentenced first. He appeared confused and the judge soon convinced him that he was; if he wanted to retract his plea and call for legal aid, the judge would assist him. He was asked to sit down and think it over.

Jim was called to the bench. The judge asked if he wanted counsel. "No, sir" Jim replied. Judge Shaw then went on to point out that religious grounds were the basis for refusing military service in this case also, to which Jim agreed. But the Judge dropped that issue and spoke of how, as it appeared to him, Jim was not going to do anything the law required. Interrupting the Judge, Jim asked if he might read his statement, and immediately, in the manner of Pavlov's dogs, the Judge replied, "I will take into consideration anything, etc., etc." After Jim had read his statement, which did not seem to be of great interest to the Judge, the latter asked him if there were any other country in which he would be granted such rights and privileges as were here, in this courtroom, being granted to him? And didn't he (Jim) think that it was necessary, in order to preserve these rights, that Americans, from time to time, fight for them? Not meeting with the response he desired, he then went on to observe that Jim was "a very wrong man with a high degree of immaturity,"-one who looked upon himself as a law unto himself; who obeyed only those he liked. He had no choice but to condemn such arrogant immaturity. Judge Shaw then sentenced Jim Wilson to three years' imprisonment.

Jim Wilson comes from an upper-middle-class background and a most conservative town in New Jersey. Working with us he preferred the raw reality of the first floor of Chrystie Street's St. Joseph House-the unabashed humanity of the soupline, the frequent and raucous fights, the pitiful needs of the men on the Bowery, to the second and third floors, the clothing room, mailing room, office, which seemed far removed from those naked needs, that overwhelming stench of the first floor (do not ask from whom the stench comes; it comes from us all). Jim gives witness, in the Pauline sense, to his Christianity. His witness-in existential terms "confrontation"-with the essential elements on the Bowery, the people in the peace movement, the preoccupied Christians of our time; but also the minor officials of our Kafkaesque state. He tries to reach cops, probation officers, judges, F.B.I. agents, even self-seeking conscience-ridden professionals who, upset perhaps at the polarity of Jim's and their lives, sought him out.

Jim was taken away. Outside, our group broke up; some to take Raona back to the city; Miss Day and Pat Rusk to be temporarily lost in the maze of industrial Jersey, then to watch the sunset and finally to return to the Worker for dinner. Still others remained to be with the Jehovah Witness as he was sentenced. He was not confused anymore. Yes, he was guilty of refusing to be inducted.

No, he would not accept counsel. No, he would not seek C.O. status. No, he would not kill. The judge, bewildered, had no recourse but to sentence him to three years imprisonment.

Rage, then, must give way to joy.

THE FAST AND THE WATERS

MARCH-APRIL 1967

Before the four of us from Chrystie Street left for the National Shrine of the Immaculate Conception to begin our two week fast from passion Sunday to Easter, Reynold, a young Canadian free spirit, advised us that our fast should be one of joy; that were our spirits to dampen, we should go for a walk until we recovered. We disappointed Reynold, I think, for we were not consistently joyful, nor did we walk in that cold, bitter air. The Shrine, unlike the waters of the Jordon, warmed the body somewhat, but not the soul. The soul, in fact, suffered from chills, neglect, poverty, and ennui.

Our purpose in fasting at the Shrine was primarily religious: an act of atonement, if you will, for the guilt we all bear for the crimes being done in Viet Nam; to offer our slight discomfort for the anguish of the Vietnamese; to clearly state not only our disaffiliation with the U.S. government, but our outrage and shame at the American Catholic's involvement in, and support of, this war; as our leaflet read, "to appeal to all our fellow Catholics to consider and to make a decision about their participation in this war; and finally, as we told an official from South Viet Nam, who came to thank us for our effort, "We grieve for your people; we grieve for our people."

The four of us-Jan Honges (who stayed for the first week), Bob Gilliam, Dan Kelly, and myself-confronted Msgr.Grady with our intent on Passion Sunday. Believing our leaflet ambiguous, our purpose covert, he was distrustful and threatened us with arrest should we picket or leaflet on the Shrine's grounds. He was worried that our position might be identified by Joe Tourist with that of the Shrine. We had no desire to leaflet or picket, and, as the days went by, he became solicitous of our health, and, in the end, respectful of our position. We stayed the first few nights at Dave and Cathy Miller's, and then accepted the kind hospitality of Gabe Huck, his wife and friends, who live in community near the Shrine. Gabe provided transportation and was instrumental in obtaining the publicity we never sought. Paul Mann and his wife Salome arrived later that week, Jenny Orvino on Sunday and Phil Maloney was finally able to leave Chrystie Street on Thursday of the second week. We were never quite alone. A couple of non-conformist students, two quiet nuns (one of whom had permission to pray with us if there was no publicity, left when it came, but returned despite "permission" for the last day), a lone seminarian, and one priest on the next-to-the-last-day—joined us: beautiful mavericks from that huge black herd of clergy and nuns, roaming those environs. The publicity we received—newspaper, radio and television—was unsought for, yet most welcome; for the reporters provided an outlet for our pent-up rage, a podium for our position, and their stories reassured us of a breathing, reading public outside that tomb, which seemed to absorb us, during that last week, much as it absorbs the thousands of nameless Christians who mill and swarm around and in it.

The Nation's Shrine—for I'm sure American Catholics in general look upon it that way ever since they were taught in parochial school to worship the cross and revere the flag—occupied much of our thought; an unavoidable occurrence, for nowhere, within or without it, is free from distractions of the grossest variety. From a distance the Shrine is absurd. The blue and gold dome and the blue and gold tip of the steeple are at first amusing; one reserves judgment, hesitates as if one were to laugh at a bad joke. Upon approaching, the apt word comes screeching forth; it is grotesque. The Irish Stew of the architectural world: so many conflicting, discordant, unattractive elements from every age and period. Truly, a Vision of Error.

Those Catholics who see in the Shrine some connection with Christianity are as far removed from reality as the inhabitants of Plato's cave. Though the shadows here are certainly palpable, they are nonetheless unreal and unchristian; and, if the truth be known, dangerous and deceptive. It became increasingly clear to us that the Shrine was at once the epitome and symbol of American Catholicism. Its weaknesses, vices, and misconceptions are ours. By understanding them, we better understand why Catholics, as a whole, have supported every war this country has ever had and continue to do so. (Andrew Jackson, who once had a mass said for the success of a battle in his little war, is enshrined in stained glass in the main church). We can understand why the Shrine, though it shelters a body, chills the soul. Have not we American Catholics succeeded in putting up more tax-free "shelters" than any other variety of Christianity? Shelters for our Sunday masses; shelters for those who service Sunday masses. Few shelters for the unpaying poor. All that real estate, wealth, and property-preserve it at all costs! For $250.00, a square foot of wall space in the Shrine's lower church can be purchased to shelter one's memory, acquire "spiritual benefits," perhaps insure one's salvation, for at every mass in the Shrine its benefactors are remembered. Vanity Hall, as it is called, that part of the lower church where all the walls and pillars are plastered with such names, and the only spot where the benches are cushioned (all the better to meditate) was the scene of a furred women on her knees, Kodak in hand, trying to zero-in on a square foot of purchased salvation, unfortunately too close to the floor for comfort; and the following, "But as you say," said a wife to her husband as they stood, staring at a blank spot on the otherwise name filled wall, "it's not that high and the lighting is good."

Security and status, then, are purchased at the cost of neglect-spiritual neglect. From the pulpit, the priest intones to the never-to-meet-again congregation, "Gathered together in this community . . ."and the words are lost in the vast, dull spaces above the tourists' heads. The daily masses we attended in the crypt church ("Lights dimmed as in the catacombs," said the tour guides), though in the English for the most part, would still qualify as prime examples of what sociologists term "alienation"; and the Easter midnight service, celebrated by the Shrine's clergy and choir, to the accompaniment of our military vicar's donated organ, sounding to all the world like a battle-field rout, was so bereft of beauty that one's immediate response was one of pity.

The spiritual poverty of the Shrine, and by analogy of American Catholicism, is apparent in all its Tetzel-like activities; the guided (by bored boys) tours, the Shrine Store (Baby's First Rosary, Blessed Mother Coloring Book, Shrine Chocolate Bars), the Cafeteria (in the middle of which stands an aluminum counter for trays, condiments, etc.; and on top of that, assorted statues for sale): vigil candles-small 10c, large $1-in every nook and cranny of the church (a small nun kneeled to empty the coin boxes every day, and the candles were removed and stashed away, still lit, in boxes while new ones were put in their place); slides of the Shrine (the totalitarian, all-American Christ behind the main altar, a favorite) and/or JFK's funeral; a miniature glass encased Vatican City, complete with buttons which, when pressed, lit up St.Peter's or the stables; a replica of Lourdes chapel, obviously designed (as Vatican City encased) for vicarious pilgrimages; or, how-to-keep-all-that-money-spent-on-foreign-shrines-at-home.

The works of mercy are not. Though surrounded and hemmed in on all sides by the squalor of Washington's Negro population, no soup line is to be found in those marbled halls, nor a clothes-room for the naked. No beggars or cripples asked for handouts. No handouts; only collections. No gifts; only purchases.

The Poor

It is not enough to say, with Bishop Blomjou of Jerusalem, in commenting on Pope Paul's recent encyclical, that "Christians by and large are not living in poverty, and the church itself, as an institution, not only does not give the impression of being poor but also it gives the impression, in many instances, of not being on the side of the poor." (N.Y. Times, March 30, 1967). Impressions aside, the church is obviously not poor, and Catholics in this country, so nationalistic by training, so isolated and security-conscious by desire, scorn the poor, who are regarded, along with the "kooks" of foreign lands, as a threat to their well being. A soon-to-be doctor of philosophy at C.U., and alumnus of the same undergraduate school I attended, could not see a distinction between combatants and non-combatants, thought certain peoples should be obliterated, felt it unfortunate that the Negro is regarded as a criminal, and regretted his scanty knowledge of Viet Nam: he was kept too busy at the university.

To the degree that Catholics in America disregard the poor-and the multi-million dollar Shrine in which they so assiduously invest is an apt criterion-to that degree one might say they are not christian, but nationalistic and materialistic.

The lack of any real community, the lack of any meaningful liturgy, the presence of the State as idol (Holy Mother the State, as Dorothy Day says), the possession of property as salvation-all reveal the spiritual poverty of their lives, encased though it be in material comfort and dependent upon national security. A wasteland.

Thus, the ennui. After a week of the Shrine, we yearned for the Worker. After the predictable apathy and indifference toward the war, we yearned for the company of the concerned and the anguished. After the salesmen, the tourists, the businessmen-clergy, we yearned for the people at Chrystie Street and the all too human faces of the men on the line. After so much money changing hands for chimeras we yearned for the sacrament of soup, bread, and tea; for a place where the poor must forgive us for waiting on them. After the marble, gold, and ivory, we yearned for the dingy walls, chipped paint, worn rooms in which we live, work, and somehow breathe a fresher, purer air. Finally, after two weeks in that tomb, we yearned for the waters of our Jordan: the relentless poverty and need of the Bowery. It chills the body but not the soul.

CHRYSTIE STREET

MAY 1967

More bugs than birds are to be found on the Bowery. The bugs, however, seem satisfied with their fare, whereas the birds, less than stately pigeons, are as hard up as the rest of us for handouts and a place to roost. The lack of statues of eminent statesmen, generals, and such in our area must be a keen hardship for them.

The Line

Nor is it easy for the men. Before the bitterness of winter set in, city building inspectors made us close down "Siloe house, " the huge back room wherein the men, having no place else to go but the streets, were accustomed to wait, from early morning until 10 o'clock, when we serve the soup. True, it was dark and dank, not well heated, often a scene of violence and continued drinking; yet it was a place to come, out of the wind, rain, or snow, a place to sit and talk. The fallen roof beam, the bare wiring, perhaps the stench, were too much for the inspectors. As a result, all winter long the men had to stand outside, usually in long lines on either side of the front door. On the left side, the super (known for his lead pipe brutality) often dumped buckets of water on them from out of a third-story window; on the right, our landlord-Venetian-blind-store owner complained of the men blocking his business and threatened to call the cops.

Here and There

Charlie Keefe, our erudite misanthrope in residence, recently returned to recuperate from his second operation. Arthur (the Bishop) Lacey stopped here for a few days, after spending a week on retreat. The Corbins, one and all, were in more frequently due to the Spring Mobilization days. Arthur (the Good and the Bad) Sullivan is back with us as doorman and general factotum. Bayonne Pete, to the joy of his brothers in Jersey perhaps, is back, and so is Earl Ovitt, who, though requested not to spend much time inside the house, is "at home" on the sidewalk of our block, where he "works," proffers his own refreshments, and, in his own unique fashion, entertains outside our front window, in that order, almost every day. John Geiss, the bearded old agitator, has been with us for some months now. When Spring arrives, staff in hand, he will probably be off again. Pat Rusk, happily not imprisoned for civil disobedience, visited the farm for a few days. Frenchy returned from Maine a few months ago; he returned from Maine's consequences a few weeks ago. Now, conscientious and skillful, he directs the work on the second floor. Edward Brown, master of rhetorical rage and teller of tall tales, is taking care of his aged mother in Atlantic City. He is missed.

Other Institutions

Most of us have evaded for another month the men in and with white jackets; some, however, are in other hospitals for different reasons. John McMullen, one of the regular waiters, took a fall and fractured his shoulder. Tom Likely was about to be released from Beekman Hospital when he had two seizures and is now on his back again. Mike Herniak, who has been in and out of the hospital a half dozen times since last summer, was released recently. Much of the heavy carpentry work was done by Mike, including those huge, sturdy, ever-in-use tables on the first floor, which serve the soup line, our daily meals, and whatever other work must be done.

But a serious heart condition, partial paralysis of his hands and one foot, prevent Mike from "doing as [he] usta." Tony, our cook, Chuck Bassinetti, Bayonne Pete, Henry Neilson, and some of the staff, visit those in the hospital as frequently as possible.

Tony continues to prepare, with ease and finesse, delicious soups for the line and lunches for the house people, under conditions other cooks of his caliber would find intolerable. He and Henry Neilson, our ever good-natured Danish waiter, both former professional cooks, are scrupulously clean and efficient in circumstances and under tensions where those qualities would ordinarily be impossible.

From the chair near the from the window, one can see the brooding John Paul, looking to all the world like some old Nantucket-whaler captain, careen along the curb edge, as is his habit, dressed winter and summer in the same wind-blown blue suit with two vests, his pockets bulging, his gray sparse hair blown back from his high forehead. He still eats standing up and off to the side, as he has these many years, I'm told. Though something of a recluse, aloof and independent, he knows who's in or out of prison and keeps in touch with former staff members.

The pantry and storeroom are kept in order by Paul, whose family of cats has enlarged considerably of late with the addition of three new litters. Not wanting to lose the mothers, Paul is reluctant to call the S.P.C.A., and at wit's end trying to find a solution. He continues to feed the pigeons at Union Square every day, although I understand there is competition now from a man who feeds the pigeons corn rather than selected garbage, as Paul does.

Irish Pat, night watchman for the Worker in the past and a man not to be trifled with, suffers now from a "bum back"; but still he manages to direct the soup line traffic and fold papers. Bill Harder, resembling some Old Testament prophet with a German accent, does a considerable amount of work in the kitchen despite his poor legs and his age. Hugh Madden runs to Ninth Street every day behind his cart to pick up the bread, returns on the run, then is off in the opposite direction for the groceries.

Toward evening others arrive: Big Julie, whose earthy humor has not been dampened by her recent serious eye operation; Missouri Marie, with her papers and her delightful laughter and chatter. Mike Kovalak, tall and ascetic, comes quietly to dine. Madame LaRoche, who sells the Catholic Worker on the Lower East Side, and two Russians-one tall and thin, the other short and stocky-take their places quietly and disturb no one, though they often are disturbed.

Second Floor

The workers on this floor were particularly hard pressed to put out the March-April issue, for it came while the appeal was still in the process of being prepared for the mails. At that time, also, Italian Mike decided that he now moves with painful slowness. He left and so, it seemed, did much of the spirit of this floor. Italian Mike and Mary Gallagan would often sustain as they worked a dialogue of pseudo-sophisticated repartee, pun-filled exchanges, finally ending with some raw yet uproarious remark, which would bring down upon Mike's head loud but half-hearted reproaches. But no longer were the words of Mr. Anderson, Marion, Polish Walter, or whoever else happened to be seated around those tables, subject to his ribald wit, his earthy retorts. He was missed. Frenchy adds to the humor on this floor with a variety of antics, which combined with his industriousness, tend to make the work less tedious. Barbara, Marie, Preston (who recently joined us), John Geiss, volunteers, occasional visitors-all contribute to the many-leveled, gregarious, moody or light, always original, talk and tone of this floor.

As I write this piece, a few days before going to press, Italian Mike has returned to us from the farm: not quite ready for the quiet life, still full of vim and vulgarity. Other news: Tom Likely, Larry, and Mike Herniak have all returned from the hospital. Serious and silent now, with only an occasional blast of his former rhetoric, Mike does more and more of the work on the first and second floors. And John Pohl fell and injured his hip, while careening around the corner; his longstanding distrust and abhorrence for hospitals was reinforced by a nine-hour wait in the emergency ward of Bellevue Hospital, after which he was told that he would be admitted the next day.

Third Floor

"Success is not the name of God" (Leon Bloy): so reads one of the many painted, scribbled, or posted sayings, along with icons, banners, picket signs, drawings, faded photographs, and much more, to be found on these shabby but delightfully littered walls. Different are the problems faced here. A cantankerous stencil machine accounts for an harassed Phil Maloney and some unavoidably damaged stencils; the battle of the "books" is waged weekly by Ed Forand; the mail and other paperwork by Walter Kerell; the task of typing new stencils belongs to the stoical Gordon McCarthy, who also labors, like some modern Sisyphus, to supply the Zip codes for our many subscribers and post office. New subscriptions are taken care of personally by Smokey Joe, who came to the Worker the year before I was born-i.e. 28 years ago. At one time or another, Smokey has been responsible for almost every type of work called for around here, short of the "On Pilgrimage" column, which, were he to write his equivalent (as he is sometimes prone to express vocally in his unique, frothy rhetoric), would be an experience. He seems to remember everyone and everything, and thus is a source of much entertainment and information. Virtually blind without his special glasses, it is something of a catastrophe for him to lose them, as happened recently. (Eyeglasses seem to be at a premium on the Bowery; Henry Neilson had his swiped from his face by a guy who asked him for a cigarette. Henry, at the time, was innocently offering the cigarette).

Friday Night Meetings

Bob Gilliam has taken over these meetings from Chris Kearns. If I
understand Bob correctly, he hopes in coming weeks to focus on
the basic principles of our lives; hence, most of us-Marty Corbin,
Phil, Bob, myself, and others-are scheduled to re-examine and speak
on our somewhat radical lives in community, to see whether or
not, in Socrates' phrase, they are worth living. An excellent address
by Conor Cruise O'Brien, that first-rate critical mind from Ireland, and a lively discussion afterward, highlighted the meetings
this past month. Graciously did he accept, too, Marty's invitation
to continue, in good Irish fashion, the discussion over a few beers.

Reunion and Peace

During the Mobilization days, we had the opportunity to meet:
Karl Meyer and his friends; Charlie Butterworth and the delightful bunch from Philly; and many others, including Jean Walsh,
John Stokes, and Hermine Evans, who were with us on that rocky
knoll in Central Park, where Dorothy and the group of us retreated
for a while to escape the press of the thousands of people bearing
witness to their desire for peace. Later on, Nicole d'Entremont
and I were caught up in the not so non-violent (in mood anyway)
sea of people in the Harlem contingent, who invaded Seventh Avenue, to their leaders' cries of "It's your street! Take it over!" The
bystanders' response was peculiar: total disbelief, apprehension,
and disturbed silence.

Prisoners

David Miller was released suddenly from the West Street Federal
House of Detention, pending an appeal to the Supreme Court.
He and Cathy are determined to go ahead and open their house of
hospitality in Washington, D.C. Murphy Dowouis and Terry
Sullivan are due to be released shortly. Raona, Phil and Sheila,

visited Jim Wilson in Allenwood, along with Elena Beardall, who visited her husband Greg. Six of our Chrystie Street staff are still in the preliminary rounds of this particular bout with the government.

Conclusion

Though lacking statues of eminent statesmen and generals-frozen in their fame and myths-we feel no keen disappointment, as perhaps the pigeons do; for where else can one find men and women more various in temperament, more original in character, more disparate in style, more striking in appearance, more at home in their poverty? Thus our work and lives go on in this strange community at Chrystie Street, peopled by the fully human, the humanly frail, by the shadows of past workers and the spirits of those now in prison. It is not the life of most Americans: the image of which, perhaps, is that Bowery Man, who (in earning his pennies by "banging" (wiping) windows of cars and trucks as they stop for the light at the corner of Chrystie and Delancey), by mistake or wishful thinking, wiped also the windows of a paddy wagon. The cops let him finish his chore. Then they picked him up and tossed him inside.

RANGERS RIOT, STRIKERS SUFFER, CHAVEZ: "WE WILL ENDURE"

JUNE 1967

What shall become of the laughter of these children? Dark-skinned and barefooted, they play in the hot Sunday afternoon at being frightened by *el monstruo*. With mobile features and gestures, Harold Dickie, former student now in charge of the boycott in Corpus Christi, scares the delighted Mexican-American children, and they scream and dart from the porch of the shaded home, set quietly back from and between the union headquarters (an abandoned theater) and the strike kitchen, where the workers' families are fed beans and eggs for breakfast, beans, rice, and perhaps some beef for lunch and dinner.

"Regardless of their fate, the little victims play." So wrote Thomas Gray years ago; it is still true. It is precisely their fate, not that of the strike or the union alone, which is at stake here. The strike must not be viewed simply as an economic matter: "Let's provide them with $1.25 minimum wage, bargaining power and a vote." To be mindful of the fate of these people, one must be concerned with more than purchasing power and free speech. There is the danger, too, of thinking that by opening the door to better living conditions and a legitimate place in the working class of America, we solve the knotty place in the working class of America, we solve the knotty problem of thousands of Mexican-Americans, who have tenaciously refused to adjust to our society, refused to belong. Instead, they cling to their delightfully un-American, thoroughly Mexican traditions, their language, and their way of life (so foreign to ours in its earthiness, its communal sharing and participating, its clannishness, separateness, and protectiveness). Even in the cities, Mexican-Americans cling to their culture, resist the socialization and adjustment syndrome, with a determination rivaled only by the Orientals of a generation ago.

The strike is more than a strike. It is a "search," as Benito Rodiquez puts it; he is one of the young Mexicans whose judgment I have come to respect. The search of a people whose way of life is at one with nature and themselves, but at odds with a new environment which has made slave and pawns out of them. La Casita, one of the struck farms of some twenty-seven hundred acres, is not their heritage; but the land La Casita owns is, and they retain a great sense of that land, a feeling for the earth, its give and take, its warmth and rigidity. They were subsistence farmers before they were migrant workers; living in poverty and squalor here, moving to poverty and squalor in California or Michigan, then to return here: their children unschooled and unskilled, their bills paid out of savings from the trek, new bills acquired and once more in debt. Flesh caught in the wheel.

The alienation of Negroes, Puerto Ricans, even hippies in our cities is due in part to being uprooted, cut away from homelands and traditions. Here in the wide lonely spaces of Texas, the Mexican-Americans are alienated, even though they remain in their homeland, amidst their traditions. Here is the real crisis of identity: face, family, surroundings are all familiar; but the mirror and its image are owned by someone else. They do not belong to themselves.

Out of such separation and frustration courage grows. *El monstruo* of Mexican-Americans is being faced. That is why the fate of these children, delighted in their imaginary fright, is at stake here. The real fear, as their elders know, is not at all delightful.

The Union

If the growers, the local officials, and the political powers in the state only realized what a blessing this union is, not to the workers only, but to themselves also, they would welcome it with open arms. For the union has channeled two forces inherent in these people, which could cause havoc if unleashed. I am thinking of the religion and violence of Mexican-Americans. These people retain an almost medieval religious energy, a great capacity for faith, and a willingness to suffer, which is unparalleled in North America. This energy is heard in every cry of Viva la Huelga! And in the non-violent position take by the union, the naturally violent and volatile Mexican temperament is given a valid and rewarding alternative. (In New Mexico the other method is being tried. Revolutionary Reises Lopez Tijerina and his men stormed a courthouse in Tierra Amarilla. He and his people claim title to twenty-five hundred square miles of land under seventeenth-and eighteenth-century land grants. As I write, two hundred and fifty National Guard troops and two tanks are looking for him.)

The striking families, union officials, and volunteer organizers from Delano, are facing a different monstruo. In these final weeks of the melon harvest, these workers have been threatened, beaten, and arrested by the Texas Rangers, who are here at the invitation of the growers. There have been close to fifty arrests since I arrived a little over a week ago. Violent and brutal arrests. More violent, perhaps, because they occurred whenever the strikers were becoming successful; i.e. when the Green cards from Mexico or other scabs (many of them grammar-and high-school students) stopped their work, listened to the strikers, and left or refused to enter the fields. Since the strike began one year ago, a total of 125 arrests have been made.

The Rangers

One thing unites all Mexican-Americans, despite their clannishness; that is a deeply and firmly held hatred of Texas Rangers, at whose hands they have suffered brutalities and atrocities for decades. Stories abound. One was terribly familiar: that of two Rangers coming upon a couple of Mexican-American boys, who carried kerosene cans. The Rangers poured the kerosene on the boys and then ignited it. That happened, so I was told, fifty years ago.

How blind and unstrategic, not to say unjust, it is, then of the growers to invite the Texas Rangers to Starr County to function as strike-breakers, while posing as lawmen, to function as a gestapo, while posing as protectors of the lives of all citizens. During these finals weeks of the melon season, when a heavy investment of money is made by the growers because the fruit is so perishable, I have felt the tension in the air as the Rangers periodically drove past the union buildings; a tension increasing in tempo as strikers moved out to picket, knowing Rangers, armed with rifles (on one occasion, a sub-machine gun) would be waiting for them. The day I arrived in the city, the excited group in front of union headquarters was discussing the brutal treatment they received the night before, when 22 were arrested for picketing a Missouri-Pacific train loaded with struck produce. Some strikers were struck, shoved, and dragged to the Rangers' car; Rev. Krueger was manhandled as he attempted to take photographs; then his wife was similarly treated when she attempted to take shots of her husband being shoved around. A young 18-year-old Mexican-American was knocked into a wooden structure in front of the Justice of the Peace's office by a Ranger (he was coughing blood hours, even days, later). Cameras and films were confiscated by Rangers; newsmen were prevented from taking pictures. It didn't stop with the arrests. Exorbitant bond was set; charges left unmade; strikers kept in jail; no trial dates were set; and new injunctions and restraining orders were filed against the union. As a climax to a week of terrorism, drunken Rangers, loaded and leveled shotguns in hand, searched for one union member, broke into a private home and attacked him and his friend with their weapons.

The union can proudly boast that no act of violence has been proved against it.

This small but militant United Farm Workers Organizing Committee, though backed by the AFL-CIO, and supported by Cesar Chavez and his organizers, is beset with difficult problems. First of all, the strike preceded the union. All of the organizing which should have taken place prior to the strike, so that unity of purpose might be achieved, must go on while the strike is in progress. Cesar Chavez spent several years organizing in the communities around Delano before his strike was launched. Here the situation is far more primitive and far more desperate.

Despite the growers' contention that the strike is not hurting them (although La Casita admitted late this past week to a loss of a thousand dollars a day) and the white community's claim that there is no strike, for (with scabs in the fields and Rangers on the trains) the melons are being picked, packed, and shipped, the work on the farms is slowed down, if not stopped, and increasing numbers of migrant workers are becoming aware that an irreversible movement is under way. The growers and their "guests" the Rangers are inadvertently responsible for the nation-wide publicity which the union and the farm worker have received recently.

Still the problem of getting the word out to more of the migrants remains. Picketing is not the simple affair it was in California, where county roads border the fields and the strikers could reach the field workers with signs and shouts. Here the fields are far away from public roads and the scabs are brought in by bus or truck. The union is not opposed to Mexicans finding work in Texas; it would, however, prefer that they work elsewhere in the area and not on struck farms. In an effort to reach the Mexicans, Ed Frankl, Benito Luma, and Eliseo Medina, from Delano, Cathy Lynch, from Oakland's Catholic Worker house of hospitality, and Magdaleno Dimas, from Rio Grande City, leaflet and talk to the workers at the border as they wait to be trucked to the various farms in the area.

On the Road

One early morning at 5 o'clock, while it was still dark and cool, I accompanied them as they sped along the Texas highways to Reynosa. Though few vehicles were about so early, they greeted other drivers and were greeted in return with the shout Viva la Huelga! The Mexicans received the leaflet eagerly and small groups formed to learn the latest news of the strikers and the Rangers. We were unable to find the other scabs, scattered throughout the small communities, but by mid-morning this small group had again reached close to a thousand Mexicans. I was impressed by their youth, their singing and laughter, as we sped back toward Pharr, where they were to meet Rev. Ed Krueger. Ben Luna, a broad, heavy but gentle, Mexican, tried to catch up on his sleep; but Magdaleno would periodically disturb him by tickling his moustache. Benito slept as best he could with a copy of El Malcriado held up to his face.

But there are other places at which the Mexicans cross over which cannot be reached, and there is the huge migrant population, at the moment out of state, as it follows the crops and the harvest. Sixty percent of this area's families are gone; more will leave after the melon season ends. Although sympathetic to the union and the cause, they have bills to pay; the sacrifice upon sacrifice of the striking families is more and more apparent. They must stay, though there is money to be earned. But in earning money there is no change; it is change these people want. So they sacrifice.

"Three thousand farm laborers have signed authorization cards, expressing interest in being represented by the U.F.W.O.C." said David Lopez, of the national staff of the AFL-CIO in a recent interview. "The original strike involved 700 persons; this has been reduced since, for financial reasons." The little money the union does have is tied up in bonds for those in jail; the union cannot afford, nor does the leadership want, its people idling in jail; but their release is often a matter of producing cash. The people are released, but not the cash.

The major problem facing the union, however, is the power-complex, which extends from Rio Grande City, with its local officials in the employ of the growers and the grower (Jim Rochester, of La Casita, for example) one of the local officials, a deputy (someone overheard Rochester say to a local restauranteur that the Rangers were his "guests" and that anything they wanted was on him); to Randle Nye, the county attorney, who also represented the growers; to Governor John B. Connolly, himself a grower and rancher, who is ultimately responsible for the Rangers' presence in the city; to the state legislature, which refuses to pass a minimum-wage bill or even a child-labor law; to the federal government, which favors the growers with large grants. (Griffin and Brand recently received a $45, 000 grant for research; G & B is a struck grower and packer; the money will be used to modernize and streamline its plant in order to increase its profits).

Freedom to organize is not "granted" to the worker. Violence and intimidation are granted to him. Contracts, bargaining power, respect, are not "granted" to the worker. Poverty, illness, suffering, are granted to him. Human dignity and praise are not "granted" to the worker. His supposed complacency and indifference are taken for "granted."

But the United States government awards "grants" to growers.

Power of Union

One major Rio Grande Valley grower signed an agreement recognizing the union as exclusive bargaining agent for his workers. This grower, Virgilio Guerra, of Los Velas ranch, near Roma, maintains that church support of the workers' position influenced him. Guerra belongs to the "old" party, which is no longer in power in the country. The agreement was achieved with the aid of an international picket line. Mexican law forbids its workers to cross the Huelga flag, but politicians, be they Mexican or American, can be reached. The Huelga flag was withdrawn the next day.

The real power of the union is not in its contracts, but in the people. The old are determined and will not be moved; the young are angry and yearn to be tested. They are aware; that Mexicans, Latin Americans, and migrant workers all over the states look to them; aware that the strike means more than just a strike, just as the civil-rights march meant much more than a march. One is struck by the dignity, serenity, and resolve to be seen in their faces as they picket. Willingly do they accept their suffering. In that suffering, solidarity is born, breathes, and unites them.

Strong, too, are the leaders. David Lopez is most competent and professional. Legal battles against the Rangers and growers, foreign to the mind and ways of these poor people, will be effectively handled by him. Gil Pedilla, vice president of the U.F.W.O.C. and long-time assistant to Chavez, burns with the same fire as the strikers, for he was a stoop-laborer enraged at the lack of change, the permanency of oppression, when he came out. Bill Chandler, who worked for Chavez in California, married a Mexican-American, and both now work for la causa.

Domingo Arredondo, president of the local union, is at once the poorest and richest presidents. With his wife and six children, he lives in a clapboard, tarpaper shack without a floor. But he is a man rich in personality, in warmth and graciousness; close to the earth, he has toiled long and searched for a place in the sun; now, as local head of the union, he is loved by the people, for he is of the people and has suffered as they have. As those children laughed and ran from *el monstruo*, Domingo strummed his melancholy guitar, joked and talked with the strikers as they sat in the shade by the dusty road, amused by the scurrying national network cameramen and reporters.

As picket captain he is in charge of pickets at entrances to farms and at railroad crossings, where trains loaded with struck produce keep coming despite the pickets. It is not a simple task to place a picket at a remote crossing, when Rangers ride the trains, trail the train on the rutted side roads, and, worst of all, trail Domingo. I was with him in his battered wreck of a car, the Rangers following closely, as he drove down the back roads, lost the Ranger by darting into an obscured path, deposited the young Mexican with his picket sign, and drove back to the highway, passing the Rangers on the way. Observers are placed within convenient distance of the picket to spot any trouble and call for help if needed. They take no chances with the Rangers.

Then there is Eugene Nelson, a writer who came here on a shoestring a year ago, invested the little money he had in radio spots and leaflets, called a rally, and stood that night facing two hundred people. The next night the number tripled. He is now working on organizing the packing sheds.

Support from the church is found in the person of Rev. Ed Krueger, a minister of the United Church of Christ, now a member of the valley team ministry of the Texas Council of Churches. Open-hearted, sympathetic, and self-effacing, Rev. Krueger would rather talk of others than of himself, as he did at the rally on Saturday night when instead of talking about the brutality he had received at the hands of the Rangers, he told of how Magdaleno Dimas, who was treated far more cruelly, responded without violence, without even a curse. Magdaleno, as the white community is quick to point out, has a criminal record, which makes him particularly vulnerable. The local Catholic priest is far from being sympathetic. He is busy building a new church and enjoying his new rectory, the "Statler-Jesus," as it is called by the students from San Antonio.

In San Antonio Father William Killian, editor of the Alamo Messenger, gives the strike as much coverage and support as he can, no doubt to the chagrin of his conservative readers. He and four other priests were arrested here a short while ago. A few radical, Spanish-speaking priests, who could live, work and minister to the people here, would be welcomed by Rev. Krueger and the union. Where are they?

El Malcriado, the widely read, independent, radical and worker-oriented news of the union to the Spanish-and the English-speaking people of California in Delano, now has a Texas edition, under the direction of Doug Adair, a former student who joined the movement in Delano and stayed with it in Texas. El Malcriado was invaluable in reaching the migrant workers in California, and is now being put into grocery stores all along the Texas border. There are two types of stores in this region: the large, modern "anglo" store, much like the Acmes everywhere; and the small country stores run by Mexican-Americans. The big stores take the magazine until they realize what it's about; then they tell Doug: "Oh, we had too many complaints about it." Outside one such store, as Doug was being asked to leave, a huge cop and one of the store's managers were questioning a little Mexican girl, whose head barely reached the gun belt of the cop. In the small Mexican stores, the magazine is welcomed and often "pushed" by the owner. It is essential that the strikers reach as many people as possible; El Malcriado, now carrying the news of Rio Grande City, will be a powerful voice in the future for the Valley workers. Now, however, the task of building a route is tedious and profits from the sale of the magazine do not even cover costs of gas. But contacts in each town are being made. Like the citrus fruit, golden in the fields, the Valley will soon be ripe for organizing.

"Kill the Bastard!"

"Where is Magdaleno Dimas? We're going to kill the bastard!" In such words did the thickheaded Rangers, shotguns cocked and leveled, address the small group gathered on the porch of the union house late Thursday night. Gil Pedilla told me they were drunk; these protectors of law and order, who break laws and employ violence with impunity. Magdaleno was not there, and, after the Rangers left, people went to his home to warn him. He wasn't there either and they raced to the other clapboard house where volunteers, including myself, stay. He was there and they were about to escort him home when the Rangers arrived. He went back in; Kathy Baker, one of the hard-working staff, hid as best she could inside, and the Rangers confronted Camillo, a large, gentle Mexican outside. They wanted him to open the door. "It's locked," he said. They pushed him aside, kicked the door open, and stormed in, shotguns at ready. They found Magdaleno and Benito Rodriquez. One of the Rangers repeatedly struck Magdaleno on the head and back with the barrel of his shotgun as others pinioned his arms. Benito's finger was broken when he attempted to shield his head. All this time, as Kathy said, the house shook as if in a windstorm with their shouts and violence. Magdaleno and Benito quietly endured the beating. Outside in the dark the judge stood by the Rangers' car.

Magdaleno returned yesterday, after six days in the hospital: his head a mass of wounds, his back bruised and swollen. Benito, quiet and brooding, is sore inside. I listened to songs of Joe Hill and Woody Guthrie, as we drank tequila or beer in the kitchen of this small house, and felt beneath their friendliness and warmth a real tension: they live on a razor's edge and feel a kinship with the searching, bedeviled youth everywhere: sick of being pushed around. Unwilling to accept the deadly migratory trek, they wait restlessly for the day to arrive when those powers massed against them will fall. They are not running, as those children did, from their enemy. Yet one must ask of them: What shall become of the laughter of these young men?

Enter Chavez

Cesar Chavez arrives and all is polarized. After daylong strategy sessions with union leaders, Chavez, in spirit and in program, announced a new offensive, in what had been, mainly a defensive battle against the political machine of southern Texas, which involves a coalition among the growers, the police (local and Rangers) and the courts.

Among the first moves of the new offensive were appeals for congressional investigation of brutality and interference with the union's right to strike and picket, combined with a request to Senator Harrison Williams, of New Jersey, to bring his Senate subcommittee on migratory labor to Starr County to investigate union claims for extending coverage of the National Labor Relations Act to farm labor, and the announcement that the union attorneys would file suit in Federal Court (local courts are impenetrable) to restrain Texas Rangers and others from interfering with the strike.

These moves take time; direct action was also needed. On June 10, Chavez and over fifty strikers joined a newly organized group called VIDA (Volunteers for Democratic Action) in Laredo, Texas, where they marched, picketed, welcomed Governor Donnolly with boos and jeers, and rallied afterwards. VIDA began as a group in support of waitresses in Laredo restaurants, who struck because they were being paid less per hour than the price of the hamburgers they served.

As the pickets protesting outrage marched behind the banner of Our Lady of Guadalupe, Connolly told his audience: "There are those who seek to divide us, to categorize us into groups based upon different origins. There are those who would enter into our midst from elsewhere and attempt to mislead us under separate and false banners in different directions. These itinerant, paid purveyors of division, distrust, and dissension would attempt to paint some of our people off into a corner, our of the mainstream of our society, by falsely convincing them that they're better off alone."

Chavez, Roy Reuther, director of the Citizenship and Legislative Department of the United Automobile Workers, and other union officials were refused admittance to the Civic Center in Laredo, where they had hoped to speak to Connolly. They were not properly attired-that is, dressed in black.

The next day Chavez set up a vigil in front of the Rangers' Hotel Ringgold headquarters in Rio Grande City; a vigil composed of the mother, wife, and sister of Magdaleno Dimas, who, because of internal bleeding had returned to the hospital; reporters were there and asked him, "Why struggle against such over-whelming odds and in the face of obvious defeat?" He answered, "We don't judge commitment by success, but by need. The need is here: the poverty, lack of protection, and harassment. We are determined to continue." When the hour is darkest, he went on to say, experience teaches that victory may be near. Not because he is knowledgeable, or powerful, or a genius at organizing farm laborers; but because the cause is just and right, and those who are wrong are bound to make a mistake, which will open up doors for him-that is what makes Chavez confident that the union can succeed.

He spoke, too, of nonviolence as being not just a tactic but a moral weapon waged against those committed to violence; of the social revolution coming in the Southwest among the farm laborers (Negro and Mexican-American) who, when organized, would change the whole machine-city, county, state, and nation. A revolution is needed because it's not a matter of providing better wages, so that these people can eat and live better, but of providing a wage that will enable them to eat and live. He envisions such a revolution as a dramatic event in the life of the farm worker and the world at large. He spoke, also, of the political machine massed against the union in Texas, and of their full knowledge of what he and union are about. He says that they are fearful, "so fearful they will stop at nothing to destroy the union."

He speaks as he marches: in quiet dignity, full of an understanding which is his, and a determination which can only be shared in by many. His face bears no malice; his smile no hypocrisy. The gestures of his small, sensitive hands are natural and eloquent.

How striking, in contrast, is Captain A.J. Allee of the Texas Rangers, who (with his company of from nine to twelve Stetsoned and gun-toting, swaggering, unbelievable stereotypes) struts, growls (cigars clenched in his jaws; thumbs in his gun-belt), harasses, intimidates, and brings his own kind of justice down on the heads of the strikers. Let him growl for himself: "I'm down here as cap-

tain of the Texas Rangers. This is my territory-I've been covering
this territory for 35 years. Nobody's been mistreated. All these
reports about a head-skinning and nose bleeding-that's all false
accusations." Of Rev. Krueger: "I didn't put him in jail before
when he was demonstrating at Trophy Farm because of respect for
him as a clergyman. Now he has tried to get some of the local
people to join in the huelga." He also remarked that if he couldn't
enforce law and order, he'd hang up his "boots and his gun." (Quo-
tations from an article by David Shute, reporter for the Alamo
Messenger.)

Thus, the stage is set for the confrontation between Cesar
Chavez and Capt. Allee, the union vs. the machine.

But such a confrontation now must wait until October, when
a new harvest begins. The melon season is over; Rio Grande City
dries up, as a puddle in the hot sun after a rain; stores, even the
Cat Fish Inn (with its dust covered spurs, guns, boots, and idlers)
closes down. The Rangers, though still around, are not to be seen
as frequently as before, patrolling the streets and "staking out"
union headquarters and homes, as they "protect" the property of
growers.

Now the battle must be waged in the larger cities of Texas-
Austin, Corpus Christi, Dallas, San Antonio-and the country at
large-in Chicago, Detroit, and New York-a battle in the form of a
boycott. The word goes out, leaflets are distributed, picket signs
50' apart appear on the parking lots of grocery stores; managers
and consumers are asked not to purchase produce from SunTex,
E&S Farms, La Casita, and Griffin and Brand. In this venture, all
of us can take a part.

And in Rio Grande City, union officials and strikers conform
to the directives of the pragmatic Chavez (the other side of the
idealistic and compassionate revolutionary Chavez) who demands
sacrifice and suffering of the strikers; and of his organizers he demands much more, for they must lead-lead in discipline, in hard
work, in sacrifice. A Tank-Chavez' term for the political machine
they face in Starr County-cannot be overcome by a bicycle. They

must be an army, even in choosing this non-violent alternative. Then, through union and solidarity, may that crisis of identity which plagues Mexican-Americans be overcome.

THE POWERLESS BLACKS
ON LONG ISLAND

JULY-AUGUST 1967

"Hunger allows no choice"
-W.H. Auden

The hungry have no choice. The migrants, young and old, waiting for work in the potato-processing sheds of Long Island's eastern Suffolk County, were hungry to begin with; then they were deceived by, or abjectly resigned to, the crew leader's cry of "Twelve hours' work a day, six days a week. Good pay!" Now, prisoners of squalid labor camps (on remote side roads of the attractive, tourist-ridden island) they are idle but increasingly in debt.

The bulk of their earnings will go back to the crew leader for debts incurred for transportation, meals, a bunk (called a "bull pen"), liquor, cigarettes, etc. Rain, which is not in their contract, and a low potato market, which they do not understand, prevent them from working steadily. Their "work" and the conditions in which they live and labor represent the most modern, the most systemized, and the most degrading form of human slavery yet developed in this country.

Unlike the farm workers in Texas and California, these men have no union to fight for them (although a thousand of them are represented as a "company" union). Nor have they a cohesive culture like the Mexican-Americans or the religious energy and political awareness of the angry young men of Rio Grande City. They lack even a sense of the land. They are Negroes; but neither their color nor their common heritage of misery unites them. They are enemies one to another. The "system" makes them so.

To understand the daily state of mind of the typical migrant worker in the labor camps of Long Island and elsewhere, Whitey need only reflect upon his own state of mind as riots rage through the Negro portions of his city, and National Guard or Federal troops, their power grasped tightly in their hands, march down once quiet streets. Violence, lawlessness, brutality, ever-present physical danger is the "way of life" in labor camps and in ghettos. Whitey, well off and comfortable, has never understood this fact; "they like it that way," he explains.

Walter—he never told me his last name—a middle-aged (in appearance much older) Negro migrant in the infamous Cutchogue Labor Camp, told me that he didn't like it at all; he made it quite clear, drunk though he was (he had been idle yet confined like an animal to the fenced-in camp for five weeks with no other diversion), that he hated it: that he lived in fear of the crew leader, the processor, the white community outside, and the migrants he worked with. As if trapped in the basement of a burning building, he cried for help: "Tell 'em. Let 'em know what goes on. Tell it so they listen!"

An estimated sixty-one thousand migrants are on the move on the East Coast alone; of that number some sixteen-thousand eventually find their way to Long Island, the last stop on the trek. They come from Florida, Georgia, Alabama, Mississippi, Louisiana, North and South Carolina, Arkansas and Virginia. Others, obtained to fill labor-camp quotas, come from Skid Row in Philadelphia or the Bowery in New York City. The Bowery men are shanghaied, transported to the Island, usually found useless, and abandoned. The Migrant Division of the New York Employment Service, part of the state's "system perpetuity" program, also recruits workers: "Mr. S. of the New York State Department of Labor's Farm Placement Office reported that the quality of crews of farm and grading house workers will be better this year" (Suffolk County Farm News).

Machines now do the harvesting on Long Island farms. Migrants are needed, however, in the large wooden sheds where potatoes are processed and packaged. The sheds are neither heated in the winter nor air-conditioned in summer. The worst labor camps are those close to these sheds; but at least in those places lunch or dinner can be taken at the camp, rather than in the dust-filled and filthy shed. All work is done standing up; no sitting facilities are provided. No toilets.

According to Dan Rubenstein, until recently executive director of Seasonal Employees in Agriculture (S.E.A.), a random survey of the income of fifty-four migrants revealed the average annual income per migrant to be $639.95.

When the crew leader collects his crew in those Southern states, they are not only hungry but broke. Before they even begin to work, they owe the crew leader anywhere from thirty to sixty dollars in transportation fees and the cost of meals on the way; once in camp they owe rent (four to six dollars a week) for a "bull pen"; meals (breakfast $1.50; lunch $2; dinner $3.50); cheap wine by the pint sells for $1.25 on Sundays, $1 on Weekdays; payday for the migrants is late Saturday night—after wine stores in town close down and all "escape" must be purchased from the crew leader. All other items, such as cigarettes, toothpaste, beer, etc. are similarly priced. If the migrant wants to leave camp (and to do so he must ask permission), he must wait until a group so desires; then the crew leader provides transportation—a dollar a head. Tabs are kept solely by the crew leader, who deducts debts at a weekly rate once the men are working.

Walter did not know how much he owed the crew leader after five weeks in the camp with nothing to do but drink and survive. When the heavy potato harvest comes in late August and September, he may be able to pay that debt, plus the accumulated debts— and if he is lucky, he will have a little left over to send his wife and kids in Arkansas, whose rent and food bills he hopes vainly to pay.

Boss Man

The migrants have two bosses: the processor (owner or corporation representative) who owns the shed in which the potatoes are
graded and processed, and the crew leader, who owns neither potatoes nor machines but migrants. The processor, like his industri-
alist counterpart of thirty years ago, views the migrants as lazy,
suspicious, and sub-human. Consequently, he avoids contact with
them and is dependent on the crew leader, who functions as employer, landlord, food concession-aire, general supervisor and
guardian. Each role entails its own profit; conversely, the migrant
is exploited everywhere he turns.

The crew leader transports them from the camp to the work
site, supervises their tasks, until the potatoes are packaged, loaded,
and ready to leave the shed. He is paid by the pounds of potatoes
processed, but the laborer is paid by the hour. That is, the hour
(sometimes only two or three hours a day) in which the grader or
tractor moves: when the machine stops, pay stops (called "down
time"). Even though the worker is ready at 7:30 A.M. and present
until 10:00 P.M. he is paid only when the machine is purring, and
it seems to purr best when the market is up. When the machines
are running, all is secondary: lunch or dinner hours are forgotten;
to go to the toilet involves a 50c fine. Other non-machine work
goes on, but the workers are not paid for it. The migrants work
until the potatoes are exhausted; daytime or nighttime, no pay
differential is employed. The migrants are non-mechanized (albeit
flesh and blood) parts of a machine.

When the machine finally does stop, and they are permitted
to return to their cages, with nothing to show for their labor but
weariness, crazed by the notion that the harder they work the
deeper their debts: lost and afraid, hated and hating, they drink
their minds away, and with knives and razors try to hurt their own
fear, where it hides in other men's faces.

The company's union contract speaks for itself: Section 7-1
reads: "The management of business and the direction of the work-

ing force, including but not limited to the right to promote, transfer or discharge for proper cause, and the right to legitimate reasons is vested exclusively in the employer. The determination and establishment or modification of performances, standards for all operations is reserved in the management. In the event of change in equipment, management shall have the right to reduce the working force, if in the sole judgment of management, such reduction of force is fairly required and nothing in this agreement shall be construed to limit or in any way restrict the right of management to adopt, install or operate new or improved equipment or methods of operation.

"Nothing herein contained shall be intended or shall be considered as a waiver of any of the usual inherent, and fundamental rights of management, whether the same were exercised heretofore and the same are hereby expressly reserved to the employer."

Walter, the Negro migrant from Arkansas, did not belong to the union. He had no clear idea of what a union was. Those migrants whom he knew to be union members did not know their representatives and were no better off than he was. The union collects $1.25 per week from its members.

Cesar Chavez recently expressed his concern over the migrant situation on Long Island; he found the poverty and squalor worse than in California. Mention of Chavez' name or the United Farm Workers Organizing Committee's attempts to alleviate the suffering and oppression of farm workers causes the white power structure–from politician to crew leader—to wince and hastily explain that the situation is far different in the East than in the West.

The S.E.A.

Originally conceived as an educative program in skills for workers leaving migrancy, this federally funded program, under the directorship of Dan Rubenstein, has expanded to the point where its professional migrant staff is addressing itself to the immediate, practical needs (of every sort from clothing and homes to recreation) of workers coming out of the camps to find jobs elsewhere. As Mr.Rubenstein told the Rural Development Subcommittee of the House of Representatives: "The system contains no singular element of positive strength for the amelioration or alleviation of the ills and destruction it causes. The system must be changed radically."

Unfortunately, Mr.Rubenstein has left S.E.A. for a post at Brandeis University. He has left behind however, a competent and dedicated staff, who are meeting the needs of an impressive number of migrants. Unlike the county or state agencies, to which the worker looks in vain for help, the S.E.A. regards the whole person and is dedicated to serve him and him only. "We have no conflict of interests," says Mr.Rubenstein.

But after all, the number of workers escaping from migrancy is negligible. The camps are filled with Walters: prisoners and slaves of a system. They are illiterate, alienated, forgotten even by members of their own race, who seek power in the cities and find corruption in their hands. They are exploited by white processors and Negro crew leaders: when their unsteady, unguaranteed work suddenly ends, they find themselves at the mercy of an indifferent, if not hostile, white community and agencies not geared for their immediate needs. The hungry, again, have no choice.

But the sheds are packaging potatoes at a tremendous rate as the potato market rises. Money is being made. The economy of Long Island receives its annual boost.

CHRYSTIE STREET

JULY-AUGUST 1967

Dennis the Menace slapped him out the front door. He staggered back and ended up in the gutter. Mustering what was left of his faculties, the Bowery Man came back in a parody of a boxer's stance and gesture. He was slapped again. Then he offered his hand to Dennis to shake and, with the mute movement of his fingers to his mouth, bummed the cigarette which had not left Dennis' lips all the while. Receiving it, he turned and stumbled off.

Though a white man, his face and what of his body was exposed by his "ragged and windowed nakedness" were all but black with the dirt and filth of his long drunk. Always ready to fight, and increasingly violent as the days went by, he would give Mary Gallagan and others a hard time as they sat near the front door of our Chrystie Street house. If a staff member was present, he could usually be "talked" away; but on this occasion Dennis, who recently returned to us, took the matter into his own hands.

Such is violence on the Bowery: short-lived, thoughtless, and followed by its opposite, a strange and ephemeral comradeship. The man who punched Hugh Madden outside the Worker one day did not realize it a moment later, apologized, and received Hugh's "God bless" gratefully.

It is amid rumors of riot—a violence of a different sort—that we write now. Rumor's wagging tongue and the sight of more and more cops, patrolling the Puerto Rican neighborhood, give spirit and body to the news media's grim image.

Loss—not the result of violence, however—besets us here. Bob

Gilliam has returned to Minnesota, where he is to be sentenced on August 14th for draft refusal. British Broadcasting Company television followed him out for the story. In our society a man who refuses to kill is news. Phil Maloney, his wife and child have left for the University of Toronto, where he is going to continue his Russian studies and eventually teach the subject. They recently visited Felix and Maureen McGowan in Puerto Rico and hope to be, along with Raona Wilson, with Bob in Minnesota when he is sentenced.

Tom Hoey and Dan Kelly are still away in the West. The bed bugs, however, are feasting on the two remaining summer volunteers, Jonathan Bell and John Donohue. Other summer people— Pat Vaught, Charlie Corso, Arlene Schmidt have left also. They helped Cathy Grant in the kitchen, gave out clothes, and waited on the soup line. We are grateful for their help.

Tony, our cook, is due for a three-week leave of absence, and Charlie Keefe, lately returned from the farm, will, we hope, once again make his famous soups.

If it isn't jail, it's marriage that takes the young away and leaves the old behind. Vince Maefsky and Christine Bove, soon to be married, will leave shortly for Oklahoma, where Vince will do graduate work at the University. Vince, with the backing of his department head and the American Civil Liberties Union, already plans to challenge the loyalty oath.

Those Who Remain

As established as the soup line, as unchanging as the weakness they hope to combat, the A.A. meetings go on every Thursday night, under the direction of a member of the CW family who has offered encouragement and hope for several years.

Mike Herniak, who recently endured a mugging and robbery ("I let 'em take what they wanted") has left for Camp La Guardia, where he has a job as night watchman. Arthur Sullivan is there also. John Pohl is still in the hospital undergoing multiple operations, and young

Larry, who could not be persuaded to enter the hospital, later felt so bad that he had the clerk of his flophouse call the cops for an ambulance; but he was sent back the next day, having had his head pointlessly X-rayed and some pills dropped in his hand.

Joe Monroe and his wife came down from Tivoli and stayed for supper. The visit excited Smokey Joe, for Joe Monroe brought back many memories of old times and old faces.

There has been little for the second-floor crew to do of late, for we've not had a July issue of the paper. Frenchie has everything ready for this issue, however, and awaits Tom Hoey's return. Gordon McCarthy and Preston will now have Phil's chore of running off the many-thousand stenciled addresses on that crazy machine. The old timers, Walter Kerell and Ed Forand, continue to do the paper work that others find distasteful.

Cats

The cat problem had reached such dimensions that some feared the Board of Health might shut us down were the cats permitted to remain. Unbeknownst to Paul, the S.P.C.A. was called and nine of the cats removed. That left only four. Then a lady, cat-box in hand, came and insisted that her cat take refuge here a few days. Three weeks later the cat is still with us. Paul's wrath remains unassuaged.

Nicole d'Entremont, whose store-front children's center has been in operation all summer on First Street, Raona Wilson and Nathan, were going to visit Nicole's parents in Feasterville, Pennsylvania, this past weekend; but rumors of riot kept them in town; for, if one did occur, they were going to take as many of the kids as possible away with them.

Summer in its heat goes on, stirring some to violence and others to sack out in the sun on the sidewalks of the Bowery. The petunia plants in our window (a gift from an old Chinese, who also repaired the crucifix in the hand of our emaciated and soaring statue of St. Francis in the front window) alternately blossom and wither.

MEN OF THE FIELDS
ON THE PAVEMENTS
OF NEW YORK

SEPTEMBER 1967

"I think when you came out of a house and step on the bare earth among the fields you're the same man you were when you were inside the house. But when you step out on pavements, you're someone else. You can feel your face change."

So wrote Henry Roth (Call it Sleep, Cooper Square Publishers, Inc. 1934) in praise of peasants. Such praise is due, also, to the six farm workers from Delano, California, who, here, on the pavements of New York are organizing a consumer boycott against Giumarra products.

Their faces have not changed. But the faces to which they address themselves—fruit store owners, brokers, buyers of all sorts—have changed. The consternation apparent in their expressions at the sight of these men and their humble plea betrays them.

The story of six farm workers in New York is not a sensational one. No fireworks here. No reporters with TV equipment followed them around. Unlike the Montgomery boycott, no busloads of college enthusiasts, no cadres of radical organizers converged here in Manhattan. The work rests in the hands of six men and is carried out in almost utter silence.

Giumarra vs. the Union

They left Delano on August 31st, less than a month after the strike by the United Farm Workers Organizing Committee against Giumarra began. They are only one among many teams of workers, carrying on the boycott in cities all over the country. A consumer boycott is the only way to bring Giumarra to the bargaining table.

Giumarra is composed of two corporations and a partnership—all controlled by one family. Some 19 square miles spread over 75 miles in the San Joaquin Valley produce mainly grapes, potatoes, plums and cotton. According to a union spokesman, "The three companies are worth over $25 million, including a winery and large blocks of stock in the Bank of America. According to the Congressional Record, June 19, 1967, Giumarra last year received in direct price support payments (excluding corp. loans) a quarter of a million dollars. Giumarra also benefits by a heavily subsidized irrigation project which brings water to the area of its farms and makes pumping cheaper. Giumarra reaps cash from 27% oil depletion allowance, for it holds a one-sixth interest in the many leased oil wells on its properties. Giumarra claims to have each year 2,000 carloads of this over 8,000 acres in grapes. It ships crop to markets throughout the United States."

The management of Giumarra has refused to consent to any election among its workers, failed to meet with the union, and ignored attempts of the California state conciliation service to set up collective bargaining sessions. "The union" the spokesman said, "is unable to file unfair labor practice charges on these issues because agriculture enjoys a special exemption from federal labor laws."

On July 23rd an all-day general meeting and picnic of Giumarra workers was held. Over 1,000 attended. They voted unanimously to strike. No response being forthcoming from the company, the workers went out on August 3rd. Within four days, the company was down from 1,200 workers to about 50. Then, the scabs. And the same old story.

With a New Twist

The twist being that six men of the fields are sent by Cesar Chavez to persuade six million men of the pavements to an unselfish act. "Don't buy Giumarra grapes. They are scab grapes." That was all that needed to be said. The changed and the unchanged faces, or better, the chained and the unchained, confront each other.

On August 31: three Philipinos, three Mexicans in Delano. Three days and three nights later, having slept in the car for only short periods, they arrived in New York, where none had been before. Their contact, Jim Drake (an East Coast assistant to Chavez) could not be reached. They knew no one else. Two more nights spent in the car. Dreak, who had not expected them so soon, put them up in the YMCA and they went to work. Then he sought out Dorothy Day, for the men needed an apartment. Under Dorothy's direction, one of the Kenmare bug-infested apartments was thoroughly cleaned by a group of young volunteers, including Kevin and Sheila Murphy from the Detroit Catholic Worker, who were here for their first experience of Chrystie Street. Our Lady of Guadalupe and posters depicting the farm worker painted by Tina de Aragon now hang on the walls, and the aroma of tortillas and beans invades the hallways.

In our heavily Italian neighborhood, these aromas are distinctive; and on the streets of Manhattan six farm workers are distinctive also. They move differently. Perhaps I am simply conscious of their moving for a purpose, for an end other than themselves. They are unlike the others.

Julian Balidoy at 55 is in charge, as he has been in other cities on the West Coast, leading boycotts and pickets in Los Angeles, Soledad and elsewhere. He was with the strike from the beginning over two years ago. His sons, one of whom recently returned from Viet Nam, do not understand why he devotes his time and energy to the strike and foregoes all his former pleasures and pastimes. "I tried to get them to join us," he says, "but they are young yet and do not know what it is." I have seem owners of fruit stores or brokers try to ignore him, or dismiss him, after he had quietly told them what the strike was about, and he would not move though they busied themselves; then, irritated, they would complain that he blocked passage for customers; finally, realizing he meant business, they would come over, listen intently, and usually agree not to purchase the scab brands anymore. We were thrown out of the first store we approached on 2nd Avenue: his only comment then, and later when it happened again, was "He needs to be picketed."

Nicholas Valenzuela joined the strike in July of this year. He has been a workingman all his life, and now at 58 he walks the pavements of Manhattan as others chop wood. Always the first to leave and the last to return, he covered much of Manhattan himself. Juan Berbo and Severino Manglio, both Philippinos, 57 and 61 years old respectively, are short and stocky. They seem out of place on the streets. Their stride is meant for fields, not cement. Their blunt approach makes store owners uncomfortable, accustomed as they are to the hail-there-good-fellow smile, the knowing wink, and the moist, uncalloused hand.

Pablo Aquilar, the youngest of the group at 26, is married and has three children. He was a crew leader for Giumarra before the strike began; in that capacity he earned $40 a day. Now he earns $5 a week and his food. He is a very large man and he frequently eats both at their apartment and later at the Worker. His sense of humor is as large as he is: with his cupped hand held out and his high-pitched nasal voice, he mimics, "Just a nickel to start me off." Either his size or the tone of his voice offended one broker at the Hunts Point Terminal Market, where we were picketing one day, and a brief scuffle occurred. They wanted him to leave the platform; instead, all our pickets, some two dozen in number, converged there. The broker agreed after a little while not to purchase any more scab grapes in the future.

Bernardo Garcia, also, was one of over a thousand Giumarra laborers, who came out of the fields on August 3rd to join La Huega. He does most of the cooking for the group; it was amusing to see him roll tortillas with an empty ale bottle, a remnant of their first night in the apartment with three of our Catholic Worker staff guests.

The Work

The strategy of the boycott was deceptively simple. The six men were to reach by direct confrontation 700-800 individual retail fruit and grocery stores, large or small, in Manhattan. If a majority of these buyers cooperated, then they would have not only spread the word, but made the brokers in the large markets and auctions aware, before they were approached, that these men were at work and they meant business. The first five days were spent, then, in walking the pavements of Manhattan, from 180th Street south to South Ferry and the tip of the island, on all the avenues; then east and west on all the streets. Imagine the number of grocery stores these men entered; the number of managers encountered; and the unvarying responses. Basically, there were three responses: honest concern and cooperation; active disinterest and non-cooperation; feigned concern and dishonest cooperation. To the first they expressed their appreciation; to the second, they will send pickets; to the third, once they are found out, they will send pickets.

And the six farm workers are no longer alone. Six of our staff joined them on the pavements; both the strike and the boycott are sanctioned by the National AFL-CIO, the New York City Regional Office of the AFL-CIO, and the Western Conference of Teamsters. Paul Sanchez, organizer of the New York City Taxi Driver's Union, now works full time with the boycott and some of his men from that union were with us at the Hunts Point Terminal Market, when it came time to take the boycott to the brokers. These cab drivers were among the first to organize for their union, were blacklisted because of it, and suffered as a result. "We consider it our duty," one of them told us.

The Hunts Point Terminal Market is a huge, complex system of modern buildings located in the Bronx. Produce is brought in from all over the country by train and truck and unloaded all along one or the other sides of four long rectangular buildings. Here small and large brokers and the dozen large receivers have their stalls; they are open at both ends: trains unload on one side, trucks on the other. Perishable fruits and vegetables are stored in freezers within each stall. Each broker exhibits the various types of produce he carries and the buyers make their purchases. The long platform, stretching the length of the buildings in front of these stalls, is constantly crowded with hand trucks and lifts of all sizes, laded with crates and boxes of produce.

The first step in picketing here was locating the brokers in the various aisles who handled struck produce. Then the pickets would arrive, leaflets would be distributed, and the broker approached. We were greeted several times the first day (we began about 5 o'clock and left about 11 o'clock in the morning) with sneers and jibes and the oft-repeated line, "How much do they pay you for that?" The broker would appear uninterested, go about his work, while all his peers stopped and watched the picket line, somewhat in the manner of dogs that are attracted by the least unexpected movement. After a while, he caught on to the fact that a picket line is bad for business; it creates doubt in the minds of most; and it is fiercely respected by others. Finally, he would agree not to order any more of Giumarra brands—not only Giumarra's own six brands, but the thirty-six brands of other growers, which he's using in order thwart the boycott. He'll get rid of what he had and what was already on the way. More cooperated than not, and those who did not were picketed long and hard. Of the twelve large receivers only four carried struck produce and three of them cooperated. The remaining one was picketed ten hours Sunday night on into Monday morning; still he would not relent. He will be picketed again.

On Wednesday morning, September 20th, the day unfortunately that we go to press, a mass picket of hundreds of people (with the help of Maris Cakars of Mobilization Committee and all the others mentioned above) is planned for the fruit action, located on Pier 28 on Lower Manhattan's West Side. There will be other demonstrations throughout September and October. All those stores, brokers, and receivers must be checked and rechecked. Those still selling struck produce must then be picketed. Bodies are needed. There is much work to be done; those in New York or elsewhere who wish to help the farm worker should call the Catholic Worker (OR 4-9812) or the AFL-CIO (880-6464, attention John Schroyer).

Now the early, quiet period is over; now the conversation between the broker and striker will be heard all over New York City; now the consumers and the labor leaders will, we hope, awaken to the call of the farm worker; union men and housewives will unselfishly boycott scab grapes; now men of the fields and men of the pavements may stand together. One's face need not change.

DELANO: THE CITY AND THE STRIKERS

NOVEMBER 1967

I arrived by bus in Delano, California, late Monday afternoon, October 16th, and, rather than call the Farm Workers Union headquarters immediately, I registered in a hotel and asked the Mexican clerk where I might locate the union's office. I wanted to find out how the people of Delano regarded Cesar Chavez and his striking farm workers.

The clerk, though he managed enough English to transact the business of room, price, and checkout time, while his eyes directed mine to a list of "No's" on the wall ("No visitors after 10PM"; "No Alcohol") seemed not to hear my question, but turned, took the room key and silently led me to my room.

A middle-aged, rather plump Anglo waitress in a restaurant on Main Street, shortly afterwards, said, "I don't know anything about 'em." And walked away. A young waitress with stringy blond hair and green eye makeup, in a smaller restaurant on the other side of the tracks, impatiently blurted out, "No. I don't know where they are," and then, suddenly conscious of her role, in a softer voice, "Ask here," and pointed to a dark-skinned, black-haired, surly girl washing pots at the other end of the counter. But I left— somewhat impatiently. What turned out to be a traveling insurance salesman smilingly apologized for not knowing the union's whereabouts, smilingly said he had never heard of them, and, still smiling, walked on by. A young Mexican mechanic whom I approached at a gas station gave me the wrong directions.

I realized after a few more of these cursory interviews that one of the many patrolling cops was on the point of approaching me. Delano, for a town of only thirteen thousand people, seems to have an abundance of policemen in marked and unmarked cars, panel trucks, and on motorcycles—all white-helmeted and, like weekend fishermen, bedecked with the paraphernalia of power. (Later I would learn from Jerome Cohen, the union's lawyer, that harassment of members and volunteers is a rather common practice.) I made a point of not approaching the cop.

Thus I found myself, a little after eight o'clock in a well fixtured, suitably darkened, mahogany bar with plush booths and tables in the rear for dining. Young men, clean-shaven, well dressed, with well-fed all American faces, drank vodka on ice or soda and played Frank Sinatra on the jukebox. The young men talked loudly of sports and joked with the bartender about high-school days. I would see some of these same men, later in my stay, wearing Stetson hats and driving new Ford pickup over the country roads outside of Delano, toward the fields where Gulmarra vineyards were, past picketers and the Huelga flag, and then into the dirt roads dividing the fields to supervise the picking of grapes by their own or another grower's scabs.

Leaving there, I walked down the now deserted Main Street and then turned left and went over the railroad tracks that divide, rather conspicuously, the American business and middle-class residential section of town from the Mexican and Filipino section, which is marked by small general stores, tiny restaurants advertising Mexican foods, a string of four or five gaudy bars with names such as Casablanca and Rancho Grande, and the rows of unpainted homes of the poor. There is a mixture in this area of fairly new split-level suburban housed and old clapboard houses, with fenced-in yards cluttered with debris. Unlike the Mexican-Americans in Rio Grande City, Texas, a large number of Mexicans in Delano and California have become Americanized; lamentably they have become like us.

"Blue Monday." I said to the Mexican bartender in one of the gaudy bars as he put a beer in front of me. He jerked his head in the direction of the almost empty bar and replied, "Business is bad. It ain't Monday night's fault. Three years ago you couldn't get close to this bar. No business now. Bars are closing down. They don't have any money, those strikers. Chavez, he killed this town. Two years more and it'll blow away."

Three of us now—the bartender (also the owner), a well-dressed Mexican who for 24 years worked for a grower in offices rather than fields, and myself, discussed the strike in the deserted bar.

"They are stupid, these people. They aren't asking enough. Guys are earning more now by working for growers than the union is asking for," said the bartender.

"I'm not taking sides," said the white-collar Mexican worker. "I know both sides and can see where both are right and both wrong. I get along with all of them. I know the strikers; knew them all my life.

"This town was wide open three years ago. Now all the girls are gone. No more business," lamented the bartender.

"Yeah, we had houses out on back roads where you could go anytime," agreed the office workers. "They all left. Too much noise, too many reporters and attention to this place."

For 24 years the Mexican had worked for his grower. In exactly 24 days he'd be out of job. He wasn't worried, so he said, but he was drinking pretty heavily. No retirement, no benefits from his employer. But no job either—in 24 days, after 24 years.

As I left that bar and walked in the direction of the hotel, a tall, slender man reeled out of one of the other bars and shouted a greeting to me. "Hey, Red (ironically, that is my name among the men on the Bowery), where ya going?" There followed a long rather drunken monologue in which my newly found, very dark Puerto Rican acquaintance assured me of his strength, of his recently ended ten-year stint in the Army. He was a sergeant and no man should

mess with him. "I'm a killer, Man. I was taught to kill." To prove
his point he lifted his sport shirt, which hung loose over his belt,
and revealed the silver .45 tucked into his trousers. (Richard Chavez
later would tell me that a surprising number of people in Delano,
especially on this side of the tracks, were armed. "You're a good
guy, Red. I wouldn't hurt you," he said, while his left hand gripped
my wrist. "No, I don't know anything about the United Farm
Workers. United? You say, eh. Better ask over there," and he pointed
toward the American side of the tracks.

I would later find out about MAC. Mothers Against Chavez is
a newly formed organization, based in Delano, supposedly repre-
senting Mexican mothers who complain bitterly and politically
(with sympathetic response from Governor Reagan) about the dictatorial practices of Cesar Chavez. Their statement of purpose takes
great and amusing liberties with the biblical tag about rendering
to Cesar the things that are Cesar's.

Superfluous Labor

Quite early the next morning I walked over the tracks beyond the
paved roads to where the city line ends at Albany Street. Flat sun
burnt fields of western cotton, recently ravaged by machine, stretch
out for acres there. When these machines were first introduced,
replacing innumerable laborers, unwise growers left them in the
fields, and bitter men, their miserable employment abruptly cut
short, blew them up. But there was no end to the number of
machines—and no end to the misery. The cotton workers still employed despite the machine (and the greater profit which the machine brought the growers) have not received any increase in wages.
What will happen when the grape-picking machines, recently developed at the University of California at no expense to the grower,
are introduced is a moot point.

I walked along Albany Street, lined with the poorer type
dwellings, passed yapping ill-fed dogs, until I reached the very
edge of town, and there was a union's original building, its pink

paint chipped and its doors without a knob. In the dusty drive lay a leaflet in Spanish which printed Chavez' ultimatum to Gulmarra.

Two Mexicans, lounging by the street sign on the corner, asked me in Spanish as I approached when the building opened. I replied that I didn't know, and, they, catching my accent, I suppose, moved across the street and left me to squat on my haunches in the early morning sun and wait for people to show.

Union building, hot sun, dust, and wide, flat spaces—these were the elements of my introduction to the union itself. It didn't really change after two weeks, for few people were around at any one time (except for Friday night meetings) because the majority of strikers are spread out across the country in cities large and small in an effort to bring Gulmarra to the bargaining table by means of a boycott of his products. But the loneliness is real.

The small "pink house," as it's called, behind this building serves now as an office building for Chavez, Jerome Cohen, and Reverend Jim Drake, whom I first met in New York City, when he arranged for the six Delano workers to stay with us. I met them all later that morning, along with the affable Mr. Kurchel, an AFL-CIO representative, looking uncomfortable in casual clothes, which, together with the working man's jeans and course shirt, are the uniforms, if any be needed, of a farm worker. An old Filipino tends the grounds and buildings with care.

I thumbed through Cohen's files on recent petitions and procedures as legal ways are sought to prevent Gulmarra from using other growers' brands; from employing illegal Green cards or wetbacks; and the testimony of Mexicans and others to illegal practices used by Gulmarra, all duty reported to the Senates' subcommittee.

Since all the officials were tied up in a meeting, I sat and talked at length with a middle-aged Mexican union member, who had come with a grievance to Chavez or Dolores Huertes. It seems he could not get along with the Mexicans (union members from Mexico) who were in charge of the crew he worked in. They were in power, he said, and he felt intimidated. Originally from

Brownsville, Texas, he joined the union to get working privileges for himself and other Mexican citizens, who could not "make it" in farm labor, due to the influx of Mexican laborers, who were willing to work for pennies here in the states, for in Mexico they could live well on American pennies.

Because of the flood, it had taken a week for him to locate his sister in Brownsville, but he showed little alarm at the flood itself. It was a natural occurrence and, if it brought hardships, it was only one of many hardships which the Mexican-Americans in that area endured. Deaths, he said, were the result, even in floods, of accidents. He laughed at the millions of dollars of Federal "disaster area" funds supposedly being pumped into the area. His people would never see any of that money.

That afternoon I was driven to the Filipino hall, which is located at the other end of town, on the same non-American side of the tracks. As in Rio Grande City, though larger and more modern, this union building is a converted theatre and serves the community with a strike kitchen, meeting hall, and dispensary of groceries and clothes for striking families. Both the grounds and the building are well kept and reflect the pride the rank and file have in the union. It is here the picketers come at 4 in the morning to eat a breakfast of pancakes or eggs and coffee before they scatter to their cars, in the cold early dark, to take up their position on the country roadsides, which border the grape fields where scabs will be working that day.

Most of these picketers are Filipinos who, with Oriental detachment, endure the long hours of picketing in the hot sun, until, weary with tedium, they return to the hall after five in the evening. The strike is into its 25th month, but morning after morning, enthusiasm is still very real in that hall.

The picketing itself, however, is neither successful (in getting scabs to leave or refuse to enter the fields) nor spirited (as it was two years ago and in Rio Grande City last June) Gulmarra always seems to have enough workers; the poor, to his great advantage, are everywhere. He will not be defeated by pickets alone; the boycott is the only way, but not this year. Maybe next year.

When the patrol car, a constant companion of the picketers, was not in our area, a few clumps of Gulmarra's grapes quenched thirsts and fed smoldering anger.

Forty Acres

Forty Acres is both the extent, and popular name, of the property the union owns about a mile beyond the city limits. When completed the forty acres will be enclosed by a ten-foot wall and contain a filling station-cooperative structure, currently under construction, an office building, a clinic (now two converted trailer homes suffice), and other buildings. And the hostile city of Delano, a mile or so away and almost out of sight on this great plain, will be walled out, together with its immediate image, the city dump, which extends for acres along one border of Forty Acres. In the middle of these vast fields, also, a muddy swamp during the rainy season, are the squalid homes of the very poor—that misery and want will be walled out too.

The week or so remaining of my stay in Delano I spent painting the windows and the beamlike sashes of the filling station, while the regular members of the service-center crew were busy constructing two bridges across the drainage canal that runs along the highway.

"Something there is that doesn't love a wall" or a bridge: that might be county and state highway inspectors, who were constantly, from early morning until quitting time, busy with their tapes, suggestions, warnings, and threats of breaking the forms up if "regulations" were not met. Richard Chavez, carpenter for the union and in charge of construction, politely put up with their piddling harassment: only later, after the day's work and over a few beers in the People's Bar (the only bar which welcomes strikers) did he release his rage. The inspectors could not goad anyone to anger with them directly, and thereby gain the advantage, and hence in the end, the cement poured and settling, they appeared as ridiculous as a flustered teacher near bell time.

Of the crew that worked there, one was a mason by trade, another a mechanic, two were carpenters, one a plasterer, a young Mexican without a trade but learning a couple at a time, and an ex-priest. All shared the work that had to be done, whether it was digging the ditches for the cement foundation, shoveling dirt, hauling the wheelbarrow, or constructing the forms and securing the metal frame. So it was and will be with the station house and the buildings to come. When the foundation for the station was laid, and before that the main water line ditch dug, every striker in the area came and took part. In vital areas, such as the cement foundation, craftsman like results perhaps suffer, but the community and the spirit which moves it, is strengthened, and, like the foundation itself, firmly entrenched in the ground, is prepared for the structure which will sustain them in the future.

CHRYSTIE STREET

NOVEMBER 1967

"Say your prayers, Man. Remember, those prayers every day, gentlemen." Such is the theme and total sermon (endlessly repeated) addressed to the captive, indignant parishioners, who stand none-too-reverently outside our door and wait for the soup to be served. The young, bearded Negro who has preached daily—unrequested by us, unappreciated by the men—all summer long suddenly lost his flock: our landlord, whose shop is next door to us, threatened to raise his already exorbitant rent if we did not get the men away from his front window and entrance way. So the men are again inside: out of the elements and away from the religious sop which so often is served with the soup in the Salvation Army, the missions, an even the CW for a while. The men knew he wasn't part of our crew and some thought we should tell him to move on. But being reluctant to disturb anyone's dream, we and the men quietly endured.

Vince Maevsky and Christine Bove were married in mid-August and they invited everyone from Chrystie Street to a picnic in Van Cortlandt Park in the distant Bronx. So some thirty familiar faces and forms from the Bowery met and cavorted on a grassy, heavily wooded knoll. And passing strange it was to see Smokey Joe presiding over those gathered around the picnic-table, amid the soaring trees and surrounded by cases of cheer and bowls of potato salad, chips, and pickles. Chuck Bassenette started the fires wherein hot dogs and beans were roasted, while Whiskers and Bayonne Pete challenged Raona Wilson, Walter Kerell, Chris Kearns and others to repeated and increasingly undisciplined, loud and lively games of volleyball. Terry Sullivan, recently out of Federal prison, and Dan Kelly, soon to go (and still confined in West Street Federal Penitentiary) were there and did converse with wit and charm on sundry topics. Spirited were the discussions when all took part and colorful the language as the sun danced on the empty bottles. Finnegan was not waked as well as Vince and Chris were wed. Then the rain fell on faces weary from laughing and bodies replete with good food and drink.

Then there was the day Ed Foley, Supervisor of the Fugitive Squad of the F.B.I., sent an agent (disguised cleverly as a Bowery Man) to infiltrate our soup line, stand surreptitiously outside our window, edge ever forward in line as the men ate and left, enter our premises, play "musical chairs" (fifteen chairs in three rows must be traversed before the last man entering can take a seat at the table; thus each man except the first one in must move from chair to chair repeatedly as the first man moves to the table), finally take his place at table, eat with relish Tony's soup, and leave to report his findings. Later that same day, he and a colleague accosted one of our young volunteers, who had been waiting on the tables, as he left one of our Kenmare Street apartments, and, with badges flashing and guns drawn, they did search him and submit him to an harrowing investigation, which took place in the apartment of our already distraught landlady, who immediately called in her policemen nephew to ascertain whether or not these men were indeed F.B.I. agents or, as she suspected, aspiring Cosa Nostra or Mafia types.

Our young volunteer, a most sensitive and compassionate student and concert artist, his sensibilities already shaken by his Chrystie Street experience, found himself accused of being a cop-killer from Boston. To the everlasting credit of Ed Foley's agents, they determined that our volunteer, though dark-haired and with deep-set eyes, did not in fact resemble all too closely the photograph of their desperate criminal. And so they released him.

But our story does not end there. It seems that the F.B.I. were "informed" by one of our guests (a young man from Boston who claimed to have been sent to us by Father Dan Berrigan) that the cop-killer was working for the CW. For which "information" the F.B.I. did pay said informer seventy-five dollars. Hence the aforementioned investigation, which proved futile. Meanwhile, we had said informer in our lap, so to speak, and what to do? At this point, the story seeming so fantastic, we asked our volunteer to call to the local F.B.I. office to reassure himself and us that we were not victims of somebody's ill temper. Fugitive Squad Supervisor Ed Foley did then relate the strategy of his investigation and claimed that they had to follow up all clues to the whereabouts, etc. He added that, in his estimation, his (paid) informer, our guest, was a pathological liar. We were not reassured.

Almost immediately, with barely time for a commercial, our little TV drama commenced again with a phone call from our guest-informer to our volunteer, who happened to be near the phone. He claimed that the Cosa Nostra, and not the F.B.I., were involved; that they were looking for him because of gambling debts in Boston; that he needed money to get out of town. If money was not forthcoming from our volunteer, certain information might be given to certain individuals and trouble might ensue.

Now visibly shaken, our volunteer refuses and, thinking it time to pull the plug on this show, we inform our guest-informer that he had better split soon. A mistake. Soon it dawns upon us that he would have to return to an open and empty apartment to gather his gear. Being busy with our dinnertime crowd, we send the already harassed volunteer over to Kenmare to put our guest's gear outside the door and lock it. He enters and finds the clothes on the line in the kitchen aflame, the small TV set bashed in, beds overturned, dressers and closets pillaged, and his own clothes, suit-case, et.al. missing. The fire is put out, but the landlady and her son are now burning with rage and anxiety over their apartment building.

The Fifth Precinct cops were not enthusiastic when we told them that we had a slight problem with an arsonist. They arrived almost an hour after summoned and gave the clear impression that a fire at the CW would not be unwelcomed. They could do nothing anyway, they told us, without a warrant for the arrest of said arsonist. We, not knowing anything but the first name of the fellow, called Ed Foley again and he, after some thought, regretted that he could not disclose the name of his "informer." We did not wish to issue a warrant anyway, for our guest seemed to have enough problems of his own; but we would have liked some protection at least for the Kenmare building, which houses twenty other families besides the CW crowd, and our volunteer's home, which was known to our guest as well.

But nothing else happened that night. Our young volunteer left shortly afterward, our landlady cannot sleep nights and has visions of gunmen entering her house, and her son threatens to have us all investigated. Perhaps squad-leader Ed Foley (disguised cleverly as an F.B.I. agent) will infiltrate our soup line . . .

CHRYSTIE STREET

DECEMBER 1967

It is difficult to write about "Mama." I really don't know why, because there is much that can be said. She fits all the classic descriptions of that beauty only the very old and the very young attain. She reminds me of Ann Jones, that humpbacked, hooded heart whom Dylan Thomas elegized so poignantly:

> *I know her scrubbed and sour humbled hands*
> *Died with religion in their clasp,*
> *Her threadbare whisper in a damp word,*
> *Her wits drilled hollow,*
> *Her fist of a face died clenched on a round pain.*

"Mama" has not died yet. But tonight she invited me to her funeral and gave me the address of the undertaker. "And then," she said, "I go to the cemetery where my man, my husband, is," and her shrill, eggshell voice choked in a cry. But she was happy in that moment. Her husband died forty-five years ago.

She is not happy, however, in the hospital; she is suspicious of all the complaining women around her. Once before, when she was very ill, I tried to get her to go to a hospital; but she would have none of it, got mad at me, and said she'd die where she lived: a tiny three-room apartment on the fifth floor of an old brownstone down the street. She is 81 years old and walked those six flights of stairs an unknown number of times a day (muttering with each step, "Got will take me")—or did walk, until she fell

down on the street somewhere about a week ago and was taken off
to Bellevue Hospital. For four days we looked in vain for her; her
nephews stopped in, then, to tell us that she was lost and that
detectives were looking for her. Today I learned from a 5th Precinct detective that she was in Bellevue.

She would come into our Chrystie Street house at least twice a
day for coffee and cake. The cake she never seemed to eat, but put
away in one of her ever-present shopping bags, from which she
would remove some over-ripe fruit or vegetable, which some Essex
Market merchant had given to her. Whatever it was—orange, ba-
nana, candy—it always seemed about to escape from the frail and
trembling prison of her small hand. But it delighted her, and us,
to exchange gifts. Then she'd ask, "How's your Mama? Your Papa?"
She is stone deaf, so we nod our heads off. Whenever any of us are
away for sometime—Bob Gilliam, now in Sandstone penitentiary,
or Charlie Keefe or Tony (who has taken a job as cook in an uptown hotel)—she would really be delighted that we returned.

Her second visit each day usually corresponded with our soup
line. Beside the seated Bowery Men, waiting for their turn at the
table, she'd stand and face the crucifix on the wall: dressed all in
frayed and faded black, her door key on an old piece of string
around her neck, a cluster of medals pinned to her coat, and rosary
beads twined about her wrist. Only four feet high and humped
over like an old cane, she would mumble a prayer, then throw a
kiss to the hanging man.

Seldom did Hugh Madden, that stern Stylite, smile. But his
face relaxed, his eyes warmed, he smiled when he greeted "Mama."

We could seldom understand what she said, for it was a mixture of Italian and English and old age. But she would sometimes
lament in her high-pitched voice that she had no friends, that
"Got is my only friend," and then she would totter and clasp her
hands, her eyes in her shrunken skull rolled upward, and the myriad
fine wrinkles of her face were taut with weariness.

Such weariness. Tonight when I visited her—huddled in her blankets like some shriveled child—she seemed all but dead. All the light

had gone out of her. With shock she greeted me—that I should find her there and with her forehead, eye, and cheek all bruised: black and purple rings on chalk-white bone. Bitter, perhaps, at being in a hospital; saddened, I think, because she knows that her nephews will put her in a home; and weary, weary of it all. But, then, feeling like some sly magician, I reached into my shopping bag, brought out the muslin-wrapped statuette of Our Lady of Lourdes, recently donated to the Worker, unwrapped it, and placed it in her hands. Such delight. The nurses all gathered round to see what wonders are wrought by ceramics and a faith as great as "Mama" is old.

Thou Shalt Steal

The old Natural Law must in unnatural places and insane times be changed. Hence our Chrystie Street house has been burglarized twice in two weeks' time, our truck stolen, but finally recovered, without wheels and other removables. Play, not maliciousness, I think, motivates our young intruders. Summer evenings along First Street are alive with the sound of sprung hubcaps and the clang and clatter of tools extricating prizes, as the idle poor pursue their games.

One wonders about the response. Peter Maurin, Dorothy says, returned home with a black eye one day: the holdup men did not believe him when he tried to point out which pocket held the money. Nicole d'Entremont and Raona Wilson, in their First Street apartment, had posted on their wall a letter to prospective thieves: "We welcome you to our apartment. We wish we could be here to greet you and perhaps offer you a drink . . ." They went on to ask a small favor: that letters, clothes, and beds be spared; but pointed out where other valuables—TV set, toaster, certain wedding presents—might be found. "Feel free to make yourself a sandwich or something. As you make your way downstairs tread softly. Mrs. Russell sleeps a lot during the day. Beware of the dog. She's always hungry. Peace." And I recall the Desert Father who helped the thief load his donkey with the few goods which his hut housed. And he pointed out what had been forgotten.

A MAN AND A VISION

DECEMBER 1967

The following article is the second in a series of articles written about the farm workers' strike by the author. The first, published last month, was entitled: "Delano: the City and the Strikers." The present article is not about the United Farm Workers Organizing Committee directly; rather it concerns the life of one workingman and the vision of all workingmen in this century, especially those who struggled and died forty years ago in those southern California valleys where the current struggle continues. Those beaten and busted strikers of the thirties, as John Steinbeck records in In Dubious Battle, were successful: their vision, only partially fulfilled now with U.F.W.O.C. contracts with Gallo, Christian Brothers vineyards, and others, is still alive. Even if Chavez fails, (even if he succeeds but that which is created fails) the vision itself remains.

That member of the crew who is a plasterer by trade is not Mexican or Filipino. He is German. Emil Flackner came to this country from a small village in Germany in the early '20s and learned his trade before sheet rock made it simply a laborer's task.

He was told during his Americanization classes that the United States is not like the old country, where one made things "dure" (to use his expression); that is, repaired, patched, passed down articles of clothing and utensils. Here in American one buys new shoes every year, new clothes, cars, appliances, because that is how the economy and everyone else prospers. He didn't pay any attention; the small community in which he grew up, as he said, had already formed his character. When the depression came, he had saved enough to last the first few years and later took odd jobs to keep his family going. (His young daughter died; later he would lose his wife). During the depression, too, he read a great deal and looked at life and work in a different way than his fellow tradesmen.

Now he is sixty-six: a small, lean but well built man with great, powerful hands, formed by work; gentle eyes in an expressive, intelligent face; a prominent nose; a broad round-rimmed sombrero covered his gray but abundant hair. He walked slightly bent over. When he talked his hands, like hammers, drove his points home, and his head moved from side to side, up and down, as if he were trying to sight the lines of his ideas to see how his construction shaped up.

He had retired when he was 62 to the home he built seventy miles out of Sacramento in the mountains. He showed me photographs of the house, which was patterned after those in his villages in Germany: the broad barn-like roof, (thatched in the old country), sloping almost to the ground, dark beams and rim setting off the whiteness of its walls—were visible in his home, although the lines were more refined and pleasing. He did it all by himself. Then he built a second, smaller house on his eighty acres of woods and mountainside. But he found, after he retired, that there was little to do but keep the house up and cut the many cords of wood needed for the wintertime, when heavy snow would bury the houses to their eves. His neighbors, though working men and living a good distance away, were unsympathetic to his ideas: thought the Bomb should be dropped, hated Negroes, thought Mexicans inferior.

He had helped the farm workers all along with donations of money and joined them in their march that first year of the strike. In April of 1967, having sold his houses and land, with his truck full of food and clothing for the strikers, he came to Delano. At sixty-six, his possessions reduced to a suitcase and a trunk, a small truck and a dog, he is working at Forty Acres and receives, of course, no pay. "If they gave me anything, it would defeat the purpose of me coming here," he said in his German accent. He's learning Spanish and that, too, comes over with a strange guttural sound.

The unions in the old country, he said, were political organizations; in this country they want higher wages and are out for Number One. He was tired of that scene; he had lived in it for forty years and he now was "correcting all that."

I joined him that last week of my stay and shared the small rooms that he lived in. He took an intelligent interest in the breakfast foods he ate and the water he drank: natural foods and water from the mountains. The water in Delano, as a recent scandal there bears witness, has in it nitrates and other chemicals dangerous to human health but evidently great for the growers' fields and crops.

He liked the work, even the digging of ditches and shoveling of dirt; for it was "useful" and carried on in any easy, non-frantic way, so unlike the work one did for money or against time.

At noon I would quit painting and join him and the others as they left for the Filipino hall, where lunch would be waiting for us. Two kinds of rice, Spanish and plain; some form of meat (chicken legs, breasts; spare ribs, etc.) or fish; soup which was always good even though you recognized yesterday's meat in it; tortillas and other Mexican foods along with Filipino dishes, which were foreign to the taste, but good after one grew accustomed to them— all were waiting in their pots for us in the small rectangular dining room.

The Filipinos, even more than their lunches, were a delight at those times, after the sun and the work and before the next shift began; for they are a charming and happy people. The women who prepared the meals were always laughing and playing and, when the clothes were to be given out, the men, not the kids, would playfully prepare for the race to them, run it, and then let the women search and discover their needs.

Emil, like all of us, enjoyed their company; he got on well with the rank and file and shared their enthusiasm, yet from a different perspective and with a keen insight into the workings of unions. When the 73 year old Filipino carpenter, "Candy" as he

was called, failed to show for work two days in a row, Emil, Mae-
stro the mason and myself, bumped and jogged along the back
roads in search of the shack in which he lived. Emil wanted to be
assured that Candy was not ill.

At night he would describe his village to me and tell me of
how it was before the war; we would discuss politics or religion;
the privileged and the oppressed. He would work for the union as
long as there was a job. He was, at sixty-six years of age, a free man.
I confess, he made all kinds of sense to me.

CHRYSTIE STREET

JANUARY 1968

"May I never see another one," said Mike Herniak, as he swerved, tall and partially paralyzed in one leg, like some rudderless ship his battered, grimy, stuffed with rags and newspaper-swollen overcoat, into our kitchen Christmas morning. As always, Mike's declamation was appropriate and pointed. Not only is it true to say of him that he feeds on death, but that death—in cold and pain, in filth and squalor, in loneliness and abandon—feeds on the men of the Bowery. As I write, it is reported to me that in the basement of the old brownstone in which "Mama" used to live, a Bowery man last night in 5-degree weather died from exposure. It is only fitting that at the southern end of this Via Dolorosa one finds the "Tombs" (city jail) and the morgue.

It is about 8:30 Tuesday night, the 9th of January. Dennis Ward and I have just returned from the Office of the Medical Examiner—a euphemism for that morgue on 30th Street and 1st Avenue, where unidentified dead bodies picked up on the streets of Manhattan are taken. "Case No. 294; Male; White; approx. 54 years old; picked up in front of 22 Spring Street, N.Y.C.; 8 Jan. 1968; unidentified."

Irish Pat McGowan is dead.

A young night clerk told us that all the office workers had left. It was an inconvenient time to identify the dead. After 9 and before 5 o'clock was ideal. But we happened to meet the medical director (I suppose) himself, as he was leaving the building, and he intervened for us; hence, as a personal favor, we were told, I would be allowed to see the body for conditional identification, since the clerk, being new there, did not know how to fill out the forms. The clerk had recently returned (wounded) from Viet Nam, and he was somewhat nervous, as he chatted and smoked with us in the lobby, before making his first descent to that most modern of morgues, where the walls are lined with lockers much like those in bus stations. He was worried about my reaction, for decomposition had set in. I assured him I was sufficiently acquainted with death. He remarked, "It can't be any worse than the dead Viet Cong." Dennis, being older and far more acquainted with death, was not permitted to descend for fear of a heart attack.

Irish Pat, born and raised in the mountains of Western Ireland, deserted the English Army and joined the Irish Republican Army. He fought in the Battle of the Four Courts in Dublin during Easter Week and then in the Irish Civil War. We are uncertain of his life in America before he comes to the CW. Some say a prison guard; others, a trolley car operator. He had been with the CW since Staten Island days. Always somewhat belligerent, though harmless, he mellowed considerably toward Christmas time.

Bayonne Pete, who had been with the CW since before World War II, died the morning of Christmas Eve. On that day, also, one year ago Nick the Waiter died. The metaphysical mysteries that permeate life on the Bowery are all the more real and raw during this time of tinsel and general gaiety.

Chuck Bassinette, a longtime friend of both Irish Pat and Pete, told me that Pete was in pretty bad shape, and, when I went to him, in the apartment he shared with Smokey Joe and Whiskers, and found him swollen in belly and yellow and bloated in the face, it was clear that he was near the end. It was Chuck, too, who was told upon visiting the hospital that one of Pete's brothers had left orders that only immediate family could visit Pete. But people from the house continued, day after day, to try to see him.

George Johnson, that international hiker and CW Man-about-Town, visited us just before Christmas and spent hours trying to find Pete in Bellevue. George possesses the art of being accepted as an equal by everybody—Bowery Man or professional; hence he enlisted the aid of the headman at Bellevue and both wandered the wards in search of Pete. We finally learned on the morning of Christmas Eve (from another brother, who came by later with a 20-pound turkey for us) that he had died in a different hospital.

Tom Likely has spent the holidays in the hospital, although he went there much against his will. Only by taking advantage of one of his ever more frequent and violent seizures were we able to get the ambulance here and have him committed. The ulcerous sores on his leg were aggravated by an inexplicable burn. His leg is set in a removable cast, he is receiving oxygen directly to the lungs, and his face gives the impression that the mortician had already "set" it.

When Chuck returned from "viewing" Pete for the last time, he was quite disturbed, for he could not recognize his friend.

Earl Ovitt received 3rd degree burns on ten per cent of his body when a valve on a steam pipe, direct from the furnace which he was trying to fix, burst. He, too, is hospitalized. Both Earl and Tom Likely sing the old songs, Earl's "Hello Dolly," in fact, serves as both his entrance and (sometimes by request) his exit lines. He keeps up three buildings on our street, plus doing odd jobs of hauling by carts, which are appropriated in his own fashion. After supper one evening, Earl, Tom, Dennis the Menace, Frances Fur Piece (who is also hospitalized and possibly in danger of losing that leg, whose ulcerous green and golden sores so long remained untended and open for the world to view), Missouri Marie, and an unidentifiable woman (who slept most of the early winter on benches at South Ferry)—entertained us all with a barbershop session that was sheer delight. First the girls and then the men would sing; then all together under the direction of Dennis.

On Christmas Eve we had our traditional Christmas party with gifts and fruit, pie, jellies, and singing. Some seldom seen faces appeared (the lovely Kathy Nackowski from Salt Lake City among them) and some regular ones were missing, for other forms of cheer were being offered elsewhere on the Bowery. A sad time was had by all. Then a group of us left for the Women's House of Detention, where we traditionally sing carols to the women behind the darkened, barred windows. The cop on the beat silently nodded his approval, but the captain in charge of the prison sent out a guard to ask us to leave. We refused, for the girls were singing and shouting from the windows; some waved handkerchiefs, others began songs and we joined them. After we had circled the building, singing to each side, the captain herself emerged, assured us she was a good Catholic and went to Mass every Sunday and told us again to leave, for all the girls were crying hysterically and it was all our fault. By this time, we had attracted not only those who sympathize with us, but assorted eccentrics, a few holiday drunks, and, as always, natural born leaders, who, seeing two or three gathered together, feel called upon to assert themselves. At this point, the "personalist" in me, to use the Worker's expression, rebels and I think (to put it poorly but alliteratively) that any group more than me is a mob.

We received a long Christmas letter from Bob Gilliam that was so full of good things that it was unprintable. Both he and Jim Wilson, as well as many others in jail, were much on everyone's mind during Christmas time. Mike Herniak speaks for all of us: "How is Bob Gilliam? And Jimmy Wilson?" he asked me. "I would rather be dead. That is a living death. But they'll adjust to it. And those who put him there, their time will come. The mill of the gods grinds slowly, but to a fine point." And his face could not contain his emotion.

On Christmas Day the Puerto Rican kids from around the corner put on a skit for us on our second floor. Based on the Charlie Brown comic strip, it was actually a play within a play within a larger play—the last being a beautiful hustle. Their skit, so the author and director (a vivacious and talented girl named Lily) told us, would need access to the woman's clothing room as a point of exit for Charlie Brown. We innocently assented. Once the skit was over, to the delight of all there gathered, Lily commandeered the clothing room and proceeded to give out children's clothes to all her cast, one by one. One can only applaud that performance.

Ed Forand helped put up the Christmas Day meal for the house, so that Mary Kae Josh and Paul, who share the evening chores, might have a day of rest. (Paul's cats are now of the size and temperament of adolescent cheetahs). California Fred and Charlie the Hot Dog Man wait on the soup line frequently, although we've been helped also by two students from Colgate, Owen Rogar and Russ Wilkinson, who are with us for the month of January. Whiskers functions as both night watchman and caretaker of the men's clothing room. Dan Kelly, George Amreihn and myself share the making of soup and lunch. Perhaps, as Mike Herniak says, if we learn how to serve (here Mike would interrupt himself with a self-deprecating "Please excuse"), we might someday learn how to save.

Under the direction of Polish Walter and Tom Hoey, the second-floor crew of Italian Mike, Mary Gallagan, Barbara, Brother John, Jim Douglas, and many others, got the December issue out before Christmas so that our readers might get it during the holidays. Before their work could begin, that of Preston and Gordon on the third floor had to be completed. Smokey Joe has lost his glasses again, but still struggles on, until they can be replaced, with an old pair of Dorothy's.

Walter Kerell is enthused about the possibility of offering classes at the CW in French (by himself), Spanish (by Tom Hoey and Tony), Russian (by Tony), and whatever I can come up with, to whomever is interested. Much of our projected school depends on who is in or out of jail. Prospects, it would appear from recent F.B.I. visitations, are quite uncertain.

Mike Herniak's first remark blasted the morning mood of Christmas. We were not at all prepared for his next one: as Darwin Pritchet, our epileptic file clerk and Ranger fan, approached with a proffered hand to innocently extend the season's greetings to him, Mike swerved again and in his raucous base voice bellowed, "Don't shake hands with me! I remember Hiroshima!"

A RESPONSE TO THE RESISTANCE

JANUARY 1968

The following address was one of several speeches given by non-coop-erators at the Eastern Conference for Non-Cooperators with the Selec-tive Service, held in New York City on October 30, 1966. It was printed originally by my former students at Hobart College, Geneva, New York, in The Review *(Fall, 1966). We offer it here, as we did when it was first spoken and first printed, to encourage and advocate noncoopera-tion with Selective Service. Secondly, to offer to those "resisters" (some two thousand young men), who at the present moment are or may soon be non-cooperators, some ground (admittedly "our" ground) to stand on; since, from what we read and hear, the voices we have heard, there appears to be but rage, fear, and energy behind the action of many of them.*

We respect those responses (as unreflective as they are) and abhor, as all men of conscience must, the government which compels them. Yet we fear that such responses, apart from principle and a firmly positive position, are not ground enough to withstand years in jail. We are as concerned about non-cooperators as we are about noncooperation. And we know that of all the doors to human experience, the prison door is the least likely to find a man the same when he leaves as when he entered. Prison changes men; it can, and often does, destroy them.

"Sing, O Goddess, of the wrath of Achilles." So begins Homer's immortal epic The Iliad. A modern poet, writing of the great man of our age, might say, "Sing, O Goddess, of the wisdom of Gandhi."

And both poets—ancient and modern—would be celebrating and affirming Man, in the face of man's violence, oppression, deceit, and slavery. For despite the violence and bloodshed in The Iliad, despite Simone Weil's interpretation of it, the love and pity which Achilles feels for the mourning Priam, whose many sons are not, that love and pity puts an end to Achilles' terrible wrath. That, in my opinion, is the essential affirmation of that stormy work. Love and pity, too, are at the root of Gandhi's passive resistance, non-violence, or soul-force. In a world far more violent and bloody than the Greeks ever dreamed of, Gandhi dared to affirm that the way to oppose that violence and end that bloodshed was the way of nonviolence, born out of love and pity for all mankind.

So, too, love and pity are at the root of my act of noncoopera-tion. A love and pity that no national boundaries. I believe with Auden that "There is no such thing as the state/And no one exists alone." And I affirm with Don Lorenzo Milani that if boundaries there must be, then let them be drawn between the poor and oppressed on the one hand, and the privileged and oppressors on the other. The former are my motherland; the latter are my for-eigners. So I, too, draw the line between those who suffer and those who inflict that suffering. And foremost among the latter is the United States Government. I say "No" to that government. I will not be a party to her crimes, nor will I permit myself to live in tacit agreement with her policies; hence, I have rejected the status of one whose occupation is—according to the law—essential to national welfare, i.e. a teacher, in favor of no status at all, save that of one who directly and personally opposes that government's un-just laws, its suicidal—for the human race—foreign policy, its unjust and most diabolical warfare, and finally, its too, too solid existence.

I affirm, then, not only love and pity, but also the primacy of conscience and the necessity—for intellectual and moral integ-rity—of acting on principle. Holding the principles I do—that love, not power fulfills man and quenches his thirst for meaning in his existence; that conscience, not law, is binding on man; that harmonious cooperation among men, not competition, is the most natural way to live—I cannot support this, our government, nor, for that matter, any government; for governments and the politicians who seek to control them, do not to my knowledge act on principle, nor—being in the first instance myths and in the second mythical monsters—can they act in a fully human manner i.e. out of love and respect for all men.

In saying "No" to Selective Service, then, I do so not because it is unconstitutional. I care not a whit whether it be constitutional or unconstitutional. It certainly is the latter, but it matters not. If I find the present government (as well as all its predecessors) an oppressive and coercive one; if I find disgraceful the grotesque trappings of this Great Society, which nonetheless cannot disguise its militaristic-industrial scientific muscle and power, leading us relentlessly toward worldwide annihilation; then how can I object on grounds of unconstitutionality? In doing so I must affirm the Constitution—the skeleton of this monster with which we, like Beowulf of old, must now contend.

I object to Selective Service because it is an unjust law. Because it is, in fact, not a law at all. Before a law can be said to be a law, it must be just, reasonable, and for the common good. Conscription fulfills none of these requirements. To my mind, any law that makes men murderers against their will or even with the consent of their will, and further, makes others the moral accomplices of military actions—those murderers—by their silent acceptance of such a law, I say that that law is unjust; it deserves not the name of law. "Unjust laws exist," as Thoreau said, but centuries before, St. Thomas said, "Unjust laws are acts of violence." They are not laws at all. Let conscription then be called by its proper name: an act of terror, an act of violence.

I find such a law repugnant to my conscience. I therefore choose to oppose it, as I believe Gandhi would have, by non-violent resistance. To do otherwise—to respond in any other fashion not consistent with principle and conscience—would acknowledge the right of governments and lawmakers to do likewise. As Camus taught us about rebellion and violence, if the slave-rebel kills his Master, he depopulates the earth for, in killing even a Hitler, one negates the principles upon which the rebellion was founded.

I conclude, then, that my "No"—and I hope your "No"—is a joyful one, for it affirms and celebrates Man at a time when a man is most in need of being affirmed: at a time when the majority of our counterparts stand, like some modern Achilles, armed and ready to kill. May every modern Achilles meet, not his Agamemnon, who, like Johnson, lures him to battle with gifts and flattery; nor his Hektor, who challenges his power and might; but his Priam, who challenges his humanity; his capacity for love and pity, for conscience and principle.

See "A Priest-Teacher on Trial," Catholic Worker, January 1966.

CHRYSTIE STREET

MARCH 1968

The Bowery Man was asleep at the soup table. His forehead rested on its edge. Like some sack carelessly tossed away, his body, covered by an old overcoat, sagged formlessly in the chair. Under the table was the shopping bag into which he earlier put his empty soup bowl. His partner, after berating him for always being drunk, handed me the bowl without comment and left. The pot was empty, the soup line over, but still he slept on. He grumbled as I shook him awake. But he came up smiling and full of wonderment.

"Where am I?" he asked.

"The Worker, Man, the Worker."

"I dreamed I was at home. At home, man, in Florida. It was real. I coulda sworn I was at home."

And, laughing all the while, he told me about his house, family, Florida, and how the weather was.

Such are the inhabitants of the Bowery: homeless and utterly uprooted. The past, a dream; the future, a nightmare; the present, a long wait—between meals, drinks, and flops.

Yet there is a real need for origins and many of us are called by names reflecting that: Italian Mike, whose wit is as sharp as his crippled body is slow; Russian Mike, just returned from yet another trip to the hospital; Missouri Marie, who looks with scorn on hospitals and doctors, preferring home remedies and time as cures. One night I suggested that she see a doctor and she responded with such an animated and insightful interpretation of the book of Job that I will not be so quick to offer advice again. Frenchy is now in the hospital, where he will undergo an eye operation; the work on the appeal, currently being done by Barbara, Johnny Wood, Brother John, Italian Mike, and others, suffers from his absence. Joe Glosemeyer, an ex-seminarian, and California Paul, our most recent volunteer, are helping on the second floor also. Mary Hamill from Oklahoma is cooking the evening meals while Mary Kae Josh is away, and Roger DuBois has taken over much of the morning soup-making chores. Whiskers wear many hats—nightwatchman, waiter, clothesman—and wears all of them well. Paul's cats have littered again.

Were all of our community to speak in their native tongues, such a sound would rival Babel: Italian, Russian, German, Spanish, French, Polish, Scottish, English, American, and perhaps Scotty, who's really Irish, could put his brogue around some Gaelic. There are few native New Yorkers: Dennis the Menace and Tom Likely, who is slowly recovering in Bellevue, are among them. Ed "Horizontal" Brown is back with us from Atlantic City: rich in rhetoric, tales, and well-turned metaphors. Earl Ovitt was released from the hospital, and shortly afterwards disappeared. He wasn't in any of the hospitals or morgues, and the 5th Precinct detectives maintained he would not qualify as a missing person, being over 21, not senile or insane. He showed up a few days ago; he had been to Graymoor, for there he could recover more easily from his 3rd degree burns. He and Chuck Bassenette are in the process of moving all of the unclaimed furniture and possessions of "Mama" from her apartment. She was put in the senile ward of Central Islip, Long Island's own insane asylum.

There has been another Worker wedding and another reception. Elizabeth Duran and Ron Gessner were wed on Saturday, March 16th and the reception-dinner was held here at Chrystie Street. Under festoons of brightly colored paper, still enlivening our first floor, guests of the bride and groom, some fifty in number, mingled with our own dinner-time crowd. A good, lively time was had. In typical CW fashion, the walls were fairly bristling with colored signs: "Resist," "Peace," "Friendship All," "Huelga,"

"Love," and many another word of welcome and concern. Ron and Elizabeth plan to eventually to settle on a farm.

The rhythms of Spring are already in the air. In the early evening, as I write, bongo drums from the group of Puerto Ricans clustered in the park across the way vie with the shouts and screams of the smaller children, who (not an hour ago) broke into the women's clothing room from a rear window, and with great delight, ransacked it while we ate downstairs.

Noncooperation

Bob Gilliam and Jim Wilson continue their witness in prison. Both are well, strong, and enduring. Neither would agree, I think, with Jean-Paul Sarte's (see his "Preface" to The Wretched of the Earth by Franz Fanon) argument that the nonviolent response, and its consequence, jail, amounts to choosing "to pull your irons out of the fire." Sartre is correct, but for the wrong reasons, in stating that we are not able to pull them out; they will have to stay there till the end. One does not "pull out" of an oppressive society by being "put into" such a society's overtly oppressive institutions. In this "quiet battle" (to use Mulford Sibley's phrase) one is at the front. And he is wrong in maintaining that our "passivity" serves only to place us in the ranks of the oppressors. Pacifism or nonviolent resistance is incorrectly understood when it is equated with passivism. Nonviolence is a way of confronting violence, not avoiding it, and, as Jim and Bob or anyone living this life can testify, more energy—psychological, moral, and physical—is expended nonviolently than violently. It is, after all, a relief to be violent. No longer need one think.

Dan Kelly and Chris Kearns are both due to appear in court next week. They have faced, as many before and many to follow, the questions put to all who would change our society: Can murder be justified by the state or by those who seek to undermine the state? Their answer is no to both questions, thereby affirming, as Sartre and Fanon do not, the humanity of both oppressors and oppressed, of every man's right to live, of the sacred character of life itself.

It is fitting, then, that those who choose to be nationless, stateless, and members of the human race, rather than racists, nationalists, and patriots, should live among the homeless and the uprooted. It is to the community of man that we are responsible; it is in the face of its obvious and constant denial that we affirm it.

CHRYSTIE STREET

APRIL 1968

I learned of the death of Martin Luther King, Jr. as I was preparing for a speech on the assigned subject "The Morality of Violence" to be delivered at Gannon College, Erie, Pennsylvania, on the following Sunday. Mr. Floyd McKissik would have been the other speaker, but understandably he had to cancel out. I knew, of coarse, prior to the assassination, how poorly nonviolence was regarded by both the white and black communities; but, at the same time, I was fully prepared to batter my head against that wall. I received the news of King's death with more than shock, for the day before, lamenting the ill-repute of our movement, I had asserted that the only thing which could save nonviolence as a movement (i.e. not as a way of life for individuals, which will ever be valid) would be the sacrifice of one of its leaders.

Now that had happened. Contrary to my feelings the day before, I did not understand it. Such a sacrifice, I argued the day before, was necessary to bring to fulfillment nonviolent action in America; only in such a state of completion and wholeness could the movement recapture the minds of the people. In short, as Martin Luther King understood so well, the pinnacle of fulfillment for the movement was a Crucifixion; but, as I did not understand then, nor do now, whence comes the Resurrection? Lacking such understanding, as I told that audience, "I would rather be silent and go back to work. To draw out of that death and this despair the courage to affirm man."

The Bottle Mentality

Having received the news, I hastened to impart it to others, as if to relieve myself of the burden. On the first floor of Chrystie Street the Alcoholics Anonymous meeting was just breaking up and the response of one of the ladies present was, I believe, typical of the American response as such, that is, from those not in the movement, those whom the movement seeks to reach. That response, so honest and frightened in her case, mirrors the not-so-honest but nonetheless frightened responses of white and black racists, the imperturbably apathetic, and, of course, our leaders, political, religious, and professional.

She said, as she hastened to leave, "All you can do is grab your bottle and beat it."

And across the country, people were grabbing their respective bottles and taking refuge in a proven illusion.

"Another nigger is dead," said a man in an Erie, Pennsylvania bar, and he bought the bar a drink. So I was told by a student when I went to speak there that Sunday. How comfortable it must be for the racist to be able to apply his prejudice universally! How reassuring! How emotionally satisfying for him! What certitude is there! It is the veritable measure of his impenetrability, like the whiskey bottle that sustains it, will be shattered before long.

And before long, also, that other cry, "Nonviolence is dead! Long live Black Power!" will be shattered too, for no matter how much or how frequently our city, state, and national leaders proclaim order and exhort men to nonviolence on the one hand, they arm themselves with bigger and better guns and clubs, dictatorial power over city and state on the other hand, while our Army prepares to wage war on citizens.

How that handful of disciples of Che, Fanon, and Debray can stand with their bottles—Molotov cocktails—raised on high in the face of the impending and possibly unprecedented retaliation on all black people (not themselves alone), the unwarranted misery inflicted upon the already miserable lives of ghetto dwellers, striving simply to survive—how they can advocate that illusory solution in the face of our history of violent unsolutions, of organized and institutionalized violence, is beyond comprehension.

The Assumption

There is another form of bottle mentality which was apparent during that long weekend following Dr. King's death: those who would seek to put Martin Luther King away in some glass-encased shrine. Our national, state, and city officials, all acting out their institutional parts, assumed Dr. King into the American Hall of Fame. The "responsible" leaders of our country literally fell over each other making room at the top for Dr. King. One would think, reading and listening to their speeches, that they really believed in Martin Luther King: that they, too, propose non-violence as a solution to our psychotic social structure; that they, too, in word and deed, worked for the good of all men rich and poor alike.

It would appear from their rhetoric that Martin Luther King did not stand in overt opposition to them; did not bring his truth to meet their hypocrisy; did not bring his dedication to meet their self-service; did not bring his love to meet their hate; his non-violence to their police, army, and the courts; his opposition to the war in Vietnam to their execution of it; that he was not intent on bringing to the source of power the abject poverty of millions in this land.

But it has ever been that way with our leadership in America. They have said one thing; gone ahead and done another. They set the floodgates of rhetoric open in the Declaration of Independence, and we've been drowning in the watery waste of our own words ever since. Our noble forefathers, true to the ideal if not the reality of European humanism, proclaimed to the Mother Country, England, "Liberty or Death," "All men are created equal and have the inalienable rights to Life, Liberty, and the Pursuit of Happiness." At the same time, true to the reality, not the ideal of European humanism, they denied liberty to slaves, delivered Indians to their deaths, and made the Pursuit of Happiness a plunge through Hell for generation after generation even to our own time.

In their magnanimity they compared Dr. King to John F. Kennedy, who lived by myth and missiles, when they should have compared him to those humble Buddhist monks who inflamed themselves for the sake of the Vietnamese, whom we were and are destroying. And the Presidential candidates suspended for a weekend the art of image-making and wholesale deception to be recorded as being present at the burial of a real man: one who believed that "unarmed truth and unconditional love will have the final word in reality."

The Moment

If ever in the history of the United States there was a moment when "self-awareness" on the part of all Americans might be achieved; when our leaders' eyes might be opened to the dazzling perception of the real nature of our history and their part in it; when the values we live by in this country are suddenly focused and unredeemably clear to the naked eye; when there existed, trembling on the lip of Time, the absurd hope for change—that moment, a hope for change—that moment, a moment of grace, came when rich and poor, powerful and helpless, followed the worn wagon drawn by Georgia mules.

The Slave who turned upon the Masters and said "No" is followed by the Masters, who now march, hand in hand, with those still enslaved. The Slave who refused to obey orders and rebelled against the condition of slavery is mourned by those who enforce those conditions, those whom he sought to change. A slave who rebelled against the Master, but did not seek to kill the Master. The Slave who fought with the one weapon this country is not willing to spend millions on developing—the weapon of Love for your Brother. He loved the Masters in spite of themselves. But that beautiful moment, the high point of the American experience, passed. And those who would not follow Dr.King's lead during his life, but followed him in death only, returned to their respective institutions and out of them squeezed an almost unenforceable civil-rights bill, funds, and a plethora of rhetoric; while, at the same time, oblivious to what had happened, the significance of that moment of which they were so much a part, they resumed their roles, prepared to support those preparing for the summer "insurrections" and those bent on waging 'peace' in Viet Nam.

For them, Martin Luther King's last words: "Free At Last, Great God, I Am Free At Last."

But all of us are left with the fact of Martin Luther King's life and death; a fact that confronts each American as the fact of Christ's life and death confronts every man. That fact clearly perceived should shatter every illusion, no matter what label it wears. That fact—the ultimate act of love—the giving of one's life for others, clearly sets forth the pattern, the path to the one way of life and death in our time which is not absurd.

CHRYSTIE STREET

JUNE 1968

To James E. Wilson
Allenwood Prison Farm, Allenwood, Pennsylvania

Dead Jim:

Raona asked me a little while ago to write a letter to you about Chrystie Street. It should not have taken her prompting to make me write, but it probably did. Lethargy and lack of discipline explain to some extent my remissness, but there is yet another reason why I so seldom write to you or Bob Gilliam. It isn't a case where words cannot convey what I think of you both and your witness; but that what I think cannot be conveyed by words. it can be conveyed only by actions in which the words are implicit, the ideas understood, the word, to use the Christian term, become flesh. And these actions and the words they contain are known so well to you and Bob that I need only continue to do them to make known to you both where we all are at.

So, as I'm sure you understand, I've written my own peculiar letters to you when I and others make and serve the soup, do the clothing room thing, respond (not always well) to the endless requests, and, in short, do the things that must be done to keep afloat this inimitable community of ex-members of homes for the aged, the orphaned; of TB sanitary, mental hospitals, jails, penitentiaries, concentration camps; of army barracks, ships, prep schools, and Catholic colleges; of monasteries and convents. If each of us delights in our freedom from those haunting institutions, we nonetheless are bound together in poverty and need to another "total" institution (see Erving Goffman's *Asylums*): the prison of the Bowery, capitalism's concentration camp, the Great Society's sanitarium, a contemporary Christian's cloister, the nonviolent combatant's training ground. But float it does and float it will.

We had a heavy rainstorm here this morning and when I arrived the furniture was all but literally floating. The front window might as well have been missing for all the protection it gave, and waterfalls were to be observed in several places in Siloe House. I hastily put cans and pots under the major drips on the third floor. That poster depicting Christ as a wanted subversive was swimming in a puddle on the floor. As Dennis and Chuck were stuffing rags into the gap between window and ceiling, the wires in the light fixture nearby began to smoke. Chuck sustained only minor shocks as he separated the wires, while standing in pools of water; Earl Ovitt, recently returned from New England, has repaired the window and secured the wires.

Ed "Horizontal" Brown kept rather busy a week ago applying for a job with Welfare. After all the tests and the interviews, though, he decided not to accept it. He's recently been doing much of the evening cooking chores; we've been the recipients of some rather unusual sauces and strange concoctions. He says he's a chemist, not a cook. At the moment, he's joking with Irish John, whose laconic humor was evident in his comment on Big Louis (remember him?): "Yeah," said John "Religion drove him nuts. Well, it won't drive me nuts." We have a new man with us, a "Chinee" as John calls him; his name is Wong and he's young and good-natured. He says he has no trade, but he seems to me to be much more intelligent than the dishwasher-handyman he says he is. He knew the whole kitchen-soupline routine the day I asked him to help, and he had been observing it for only a few days.

Whiskers has split for uptown: Roger DuBois has left for Canada; Paul Muller and Joe Glosemeyer took off for the West Coast; and Mary Kae Josh has been traveling on the East Coast.

But we have Tom Temple, whom you may remember from three years ago, returned with Linda Glassner; Sue Bziennik, a friend of Karl Meyer, is with us for a short time; Julian Abernathy, a tall red-haired college graduate from Georgia, delights in waiting on the soupline and reminds me of Bob Gilliam's gentle ways and friendly manner. But the most refreshing person on our scene is Joan Levy, a young high school senior, who originally came here to do a term paper but has been coming around ever since; she talks back to Italian Mike, talks down Horizontal Brown, quarrels with me, and is very much herself.

Our men's clothing room thing has changed some because we no longer can use the back room. One section of the wall of that room had to be used as a ceiling-board for the front pantry; some of the local kids invaded the pantry by chopping through the roof. They got away with a lot of laughs and a few spices.

Paul thought I was in league with the devil when I suggested that a friend of mine who does research on cats and monkeys might be interested in come of his cats. He thinks that some of our readers might be more humane recipients of them.

We did not have a May issue of the paper, so the second floor has been somewhat deserted. Frenchie and Johnny, Polish Walter and Italian Mike, Brother John and Herbie, and all our new volunteers will soon be busy on this issue. The post office has made more work for Preston and Gordon by demanding that even isolated subscribers be zip coded. Smokey has lost his glasses again.

We were honored and delighted to meet Ammon and his wife Joan on their recent visit. Ammon spoke at the Friday night meeting to a packed house. His life—rich in the essentials, poor in the necessities, consistent in principle, rife with privation—remains a challenge to us, as he well knows. To endure and face life with the joy and energy he still retains and radiates may prove too much for us—the children of the Bomb.

Check week, that first week of the month when the penniless may briefly indulge in second helpings, will soon be upon us. It is then that my role as guard to the rioting and rampaging prisoners

of the Bowery really grates me. For I, who identify with you in
principle and being as prisoner and witness, must play guard to
other prisoners, keep the peace in our cell block. But, unlike the
guards of prisons or the staff of mental hospitals, we, who guard
the prisoners here, are bound to them in need and desire; for, in so
far as we participate in, actually or vicariously, their day by day
suffering, the recurring stupefaction, the hourly humiliation, we
dissolve the distinction between guard and prisoner, until there is
no line left at all and we remain, to be remembered to you, as the
people at Chrystie Street.

MILLLER AND KELLY JAILED

JULY-AUGUST 1968

Elsewhere in this issue I write of the characteristics of the revolutionary way of life as abstracted from the *Diary of Che Guevara*, a violent revolutionary. Now I must write of two men involved in the nonviolent struggle in so far as the CW participates in it, David Miller and Dan Kelly, who within one week in mid June were taken away to begin their terms in jail of two and a half and three years respectively for refusal to take part in the latest United States effort at mass extermination.

Both left college careers and all that means in terms of alienation from the major ruts of our society, as well as from family dreams of success and status, to join the Worker; that is, to make soup, wait on tables, prepare meals, often from scratch, distribute clothing, live in the squalid, bug-ridden apartments on Kenmare Street, meet the immediate needs of our house people and those of Bowery men also, participate in the feverish, frenetic atmosphere of the lost and the searching inhabitants of our community, as well as in the activites of the peace movement, here and elsewhere, in fasts and picketing, in mass rallies and solitary vigils, in jail and out of jail. They paid their dues.

Both are reticent men: slow or never to anger, determined in their quiet way not to be moved from their position, yet full of life and vitality which made them good to be around, and great in our CW parties—those spontaneous celebrations of the free who cannot contain their love. I do not romanticize.

David was the first in the country to burn his draft card when that act was declared a felony. I think against his better judgment he was persuaded to take the case to court with the assistance of the American Civil Liberties Union, and consequently faced for almost three years a type of Kafkaesque *Trial* scene that, to his unhassled being, proved to be a hassle. His vocation, as he sees it, is that of a "non-violent witness"—that is, a man, whole and entire, who says simply, irrevocably, with his whole being, "No, I will not go." That he knew what must be said "yes" to is evident from his operation, in spite of the uncertainty of his now fettered-in-legalities future, of a Catholic Worker House of Hospitality in Washington, D.C. That he chose to do this at a time when he was already married and a father bears witness to his determination and dedication. That he chose to do it in Washington, in the black ghetto, during a time of riots and rumors of riot, speaks for itself.

Dan Kelly moved with ease among the poor, for he moved without pretense, honestly and wonderfully himself. He seemed to feel no great need to articulate his position in any formal manner. I don't think he even wrote a statement for his sentencing. It did not matter. We knew, he knew, anyone who wanted to know, knew. He was younger than Dave or any of the rest of us at the time. He took part in the two-week fast we held in Washington without complaining or losing his sense of humor. After he had been with us for the better of a year, having already made his break with Selective Service, and taken part in the Eastern Conference on Noncooperation, organized by the CW, the hippie thing happened and he went West. When he returned from that scene, we were somewhat worried. His searching had led him to a way of life unburdened by our daily grind, the monotonous claim of acts that must be done to keep food, clothing and a roof on top of us. He rented a storefront, opened it to kids in the neighborhood and also to Bowery people who wanted to break with the Bowery syndrome, took up sandal-making, and still made our scene, although he did not want to be dependant on it. He visited Bob Gilliam, (with whom he had fasted) in Sandstone penitentiary. During this time, the Resistance made popular a number of avenues of escape from the draft, as well as swelling the list of noncooperators, and I'm sure these ways were weighing on his mind. When it came time, however, to finally face, after those long months of searching, the courtroom sentencing game, he was there, smiling and shuffling off in his sandals, serene and certain, ludicrously surrounded and held by federal agents.

Both David and Dan, as well as Fr.Phil Berrigan, have joined Jim Wilson and the other draft refusers in the Allenwood Penitentiary Farm in Allenwood, Pennsylvania. Catherine Miller, David's wife, is pregnant with their second child and stays, when not visiting him or friends in the city, at the CW farm in Tivoli, N.Y. Dan Kelly's younger brother has become a noncooperator.

It should not be necessary, given the witness of their days, to state that they are religious men; that at the root of their rebellion is the Christ of Christianity, as Ignazio Silone puts it, "that neither abdicates in the face of Mammon, nor proposes concordats with Pontius Pilate, nor offers easy careers to the ambitious, but rather leads to prison, seeing that crucifixion is no longer practiced." (*Bread and Wine*).

The quiet revolution goes on. It must be different for those in prison to understand how essential their role is to those of us on the outside. Without their example of self sacrifice, courage, decision, and identification with the poor, we would have to look to ourselves, and that is always uncomfortable, or to others still functioning in this "free society" and that is frequently embarrassing. Besides, as long as we remain free we cannot be much of an enemy (so, we'll try harder) to those powers which have seen fit to put these gentle men away.

CHE AND THE REVOLUTIONARY EXPERIENCE

JULY-AUGUST 1968

I propose to discuss the *Diary of Ernesto Che Guevara,* which he wrote during the twelve months of guerilla activity in Bolivia, November 7, 1966 to October 7, 1967, as published in *Ramparts* magazine (Vol. 7, No. 1, July 27, 1968).

My major concern is to abstract from the *Diary* the characteristics of a revolutionary way of life. I am concerned with those marks which distinguish it from other ways of life, and with those universal traits of revolutionaries, whether they be violent or nonviolent, which have characterized, in the past and present, the revolutionized man. That we are concerned here with a violent revolutionary and the lives and attitudes of men committed to, among other things, violence, should not prevent our inquiry from being fruitful. I would hope that after examining their way of life, we who are committed to the nonviolent struggle might more easily recognized wherein our lives are or are not revolutionary and proceed to address ourselves to remedies.

Some might object that I am contributing to the myth of Che, and I must reply, "I hope so." I regard Che as an authentic revolutionary, a superior man. In a century besotted with the phony heroes of declining imperial states, effectively sold to the masses through TV, radio, and films, it is necessary for the sake of the deceived people to mythicize the few valid heroes of our time.

Some Distinctions

Before I proceed to examine the *Diary* I should make clear my position; for I am praising here a violent revolutionary and, being a pacifist, it is necessary to make some distinctions.

I. Believing that revolution, i.e., the overthrow or undermining of systems, structures, institutions, and governments, which are oppressive and repressive, is the sole, uncompromising position open to men of conscience and principle, I cannot but have admiration and respect for—indeed, a great love—for revolutionaries, be they violent or nonviolent.

II. Believing that the revolutionary way of life is, in fact, the highest form of human activity, I must perforce affirm it of those committed to violence against oppressors and for the sake of the oppressed, as well as affirming it of nonviolent revolutionaries, who are opposed to the same oppressive structures, but choose to confront them differently.

III. Believing that nonviolent revolutionaries are engaged not only with tangible oppressive structures, but with intangible personal and human traits—the roots of violence in the condition of man—that are found in both oppressor and oppressed, and revolutionaries of whatever bent, I cannot condemn violence (that is not to say I sanction it or participate in it) on the part of a revolutionary until I myself have conquered violence in my own life. This condition, as yet unachieved, prohibits any condemnation of violence in a noble cause, while it permits condemnation of violence in ignoble ones; that is, the violence enacted against the helpless, the poor, the powerless, by whatever means and in whatever manner, whether by military might, social inequality, or economic discrimination.

IV. Believing that it is not nations, nor governments primarily, nor societies, individual groups, parties, etc. that must be changed and altered in order to affect the betterment of man; rather that individual men must be changed and altered and revolutionized so that, once living wholly human lives, they may bring to bear upon the parties, structures, institutions, etc. the full force of their being; I cannot but admire men, though committed to violence, who sacrifice their security, comfort, happiness, family life and all the longed for human pleasures and satisfactions for the sake of others; who are willing to endure great hardship, toil, exhaustion, sickness, hunger; as well as the vicissitudes of war, weariness, pain, the ever present fear of death and death itself. I cannot but admire that sacrifice, that commitment. And predicate of them that man is made of that. That they are men.

V. Revolutionized men and their followers—such as Che, King, Malcolm X—are the revolution. The societal changes which may or may not follow in the aftermath of such men are simply the natural consequences of their actions and lives in so far as the structures within a given society can approximate the values and ideas these men embraced and incarnated. These latter structures, in time corrupted, will call forth a new generation of revolutionaries, who will in turn revitalize the dreams and the reality of Man. If one posits the labor unions in America today as examples of such latter structures, it is interesting to point out how the nonviolent United Farm Workers Organizing Committee, headed by Cesar Chavez, (really a revolutionary movement of farm workers, not simply a union movement) is instilling into these latter structures a renewed idealism and sense of purpose, as the AFL-CIO, Teamsters, Seamen and Taxicab drivers come to the aid of the fledgling union.

The Diary

Like most diaries, Che's was not intended for publication, although its contents would probably have formed the substance of a work on the Bolivian campaign had Che lived. There was no reason, therefore, to be dishonest, pretentious, or rhetorical, since the notes served, as Mr. Castro observes in his fine introduction, as a "working guide in the constant evaluation of the occurrences, the situation and the men. They also served as an expressive outlet for his profoundly observant spirit, analytical but often laced with a fine sense of humor." What we have, in fact, is a remarkably candid and honest appraisal of the major events of each day, analyses of incidents, evaluations and observations upon himself, his men, and the environment, important decisions, problems, and a record of the day by day struggle for survival in the jungle.

The *Diary* is not a polemic in the manner of Marx, Lenin, or Trotsky; nor is it a blueprint for revolution, such as Debray's work. I am attracted to this diary because I believe it to be authentic in a way that tracts, manifestoes, polemics, blueprints, etc. are not authentic. As Mr. Castro observes in his introduction, Che's diary notations were "of revolutionary content, pedagogic and human."

These terms at once describe the work and the man. They are terms which must be understood, as they are applied, in their pure form. "Revolutionary content" does not apply to theory and abstractions (as necessary as they are); it refers to actual day by day, hour by hour, actions of revolutionaries. That is, actions in which the theory is implied, implicit. The action is the theory lived out. Very little theory, in fact, is to be found in the work; but a great many references to individuals, actions, missions, failures, errors, and all that pertains to men interacting with themselves, their environment, and their objectives in a radical way.

Mr. Castro's term "pedagogic"—normally confined to university use—is properly used here to describe the analyses, evaluations, decisions, etc., as well as the lectures Che was regularly giving his men; properly understood, then, revolutionary content can only be taught by revolutionaries during a revolution. For revolutionary content is not theory alone, nor a system of abstractions; but human beings, in all their frailty and indecision, living at, striving for, the peak, the highest form of human experience and action under adverse conditions.

It is characteristic of such men that they stand alone. They are cut off by the very nature of their ideas and actions from the normal activities of the masses of men. They are strangers in the land. Separateness is total. Interiorly, they must constantly seek to live out their role in the face of their plodding humanness, which drags them down from objectivity and detachment to selfish concerns. Externally, they are remote from family, friends, and homeland; they are remote, too, from their contacts in the cities and other areas of Bolivia. What is revealing, also is that they are cut off from much of what we normally refer to as civilized life and life, except for equipment and such, as primitive men in a primitive world. In the notes for November 8th and 9th, 1966, the first few days of the guerilla stage, Che records the following: "We spent the day in the heavily wooded area by the creek, scarcely 100 meters from the house. We were attacked by some kind of tree ducks, which don't peck but are very bothersome. We have come across the following species here: sheep and cattle ticks, tree ducks, gnats, marigui, and mosquitoes . . ." (Nov.8). "An uneventful day. We made an exploration following the course of the River Nacahuasu (really a creek) with Tumaini, but we did not reach the source. It runs through the steep inclines and apparently the region is seldom frequented. With adequate discipline one could stay there for a long time. A heavy rain forced us out of the thicket and into the house. I picked six sheep or cattle ticks from my body" (Nov.9).

The constant enemy throughout the operation—bugs, the elements, the terrain—accentuates the essential separateness of the revolutionary experience, with the necessary consequence of states of profound loneliness and abandon. Witness the solitary names of Che's family appearing at the beginning of various entries, corresponding to birthdays, etc.

This essay would be overly long were I to develop the particular incidents and people involved in the nonviolent struggle which parallel the above characteristic as well as all that follow. The isolations mentioned above is especially characteristic of the nonviolent farm worker's movement, alluded to earlier, in California and Texas. (See my articles on that movement, *The Catholic Worker*, Vol. XXXIII, No. 8, No. 10, No.11, No.12). It is, of course, true of Dorothy Day's long pilgrimage, eloquent testimony of which is in her book, *The Long Loneliness*.

Counteracting the terrible aloneness is the intense community life of the guerilla group. They must live nakedly to one another. If they are strangers to the instincts of their own lower natures and inscrutable to outsiders, they are, at the same time, vividly known and familiar to each other. In the violent revolution one's measures is not necessarily in battle, where training, tactics, and skills obtain; but in living with each other in mutuality and cooperation:

January 6, 1967: 'After class, I held forth on the topic of the necessary qualities of the guerilla fighter and the need for more discipline, and explained that our mission, above all, was to form a nucleus of steel to serve as example, and in this way explained why it is so necessary to study, imperative need for the future. After that, I brought together the heads of the groups . . . I explained why Joaquin had been chosen as second in command, which was due to some mistakes on Marco's part which were constantly being repeated; I criticized the attitude taken by Joaquin due to the incident with Miguel on New Year's Day . . . At the end, Ricardo told me of something which took place between him and Ivan, in front of Tania, in which they cursed each other, and Ricardo ordered Ivan to leave the jeep. These disagreeable incidents among the comrades are spoiling our work."

January 12, 1967: "Joaquin told me that Marcos was hurt because of the reference that was made to his errors in the meeting the other day. I have to speak to him."

January 13, 1967: "I spoke to Marcos; he complained because the criticism took place in front of the Bolivians. His argument was senseless. Except for his emotional state, worth considering; all the rest was unimportant.

"Some despicable phrases which Alejandro had used against
him were mentioned. This was cleared up and it appears as though
there were no bad intentions, nothing except a little gossip. Marcos
calmed down a little."

Nor are the dead absolved from judgment:

July 31, 1967: "Of our dead, it is difficult to catalog Raul due
to his introspection; he was not much of a fighter or worker . . .
Ricardo was the most undisciplined of the Cuban group and the
one with the least determination to face everyday sacrifice . . ."

As constant as Che's allusions to lack of contact with others in
the movement, are his references to the "everyday sacrifices" demanded of members, together with criticisms of what might appear to the outsider as minor faults: on May 11, 1967, Che makes
the notation: "I must talk seriously with Benigno and Urbano, for
the former ate a can of fish on the day of the battle but denied it,
and Urbano ate part of the *chaqui* at Rubio's camp." On April 14,
1967, the notation appears: "Canned milk was brought from the
upper cave: 23 cans had disappeared mysteriously. Moro had left
48, and nobody seems to have had time to remove them. Milk is
one of our corrupting factors."

It becomes apparent that there are no minor faults nor minor
activities in the life of a revolutionary. The least of things is of
major importance. Whatever does not contribute to the unity of
the group, no matter how petty, is to be rooted out, by punishment if necessary; for each fault betrays a lack of discipline and
responsibility. Besides, it is essential to set an "example" not only
to others in the group, but to the peasants (indeed, the world at
large) who must admire and have confidence in those whom they
are expected to follow.

As Mr. Castro points out: "The formation of a guerrilla is a
constant call to the conscience and honor of every man. Che knew
how to touch on the most sensitive fibers of the revolutionaries.
When Marcos, repeatedly admonished by Che, was warned that
he could be dishonorably discharged from the guerrillas, he said,
'First I must be shot!' Later on he gave his life heroically. The

behavior of all the men in whom Che put his confidence and whom he had to admonish for some reason or another during the course of the struggle was similar. He was a fraternal and human chief who also knew how to be exacting and occasionally even severe, but above all, and even more so than with the others, Che was severe upon himself. He based the discipline of the guerrilla on their moral conscience and on the tremendous force of his own personal example."

Such are the roots of the revolutionary community: conscience and honor. Conscience and honor not only on a theoretical plane, in relation to causes and ideologies; but more importantly, I think, on the level of sardines and canned milk. For the totality of the revolutionary experience is such that its spirit must pervade the animosities, grudges, disputes, and petty jealousies of individual members. The issues here are not theoretical nor even tactical ones; they are human ones: the nitty gritty demands of life in an intense community.

The *Diary* effectively dispels one of the prevailing myths about revolutionary life; i.e., that it is romantic, exciting, exhilarating. Instead, we find it consists of hardship, denial, hard work, sacrifice, long hours, even days of inactivity. No talk of victories is to be found here; rather daily accounts of the search for food, periods of hunger, bitter water, and when no water was available urine sufficed, and illness followed. Little of the dramatic is to be found; nothing spectacular. A typical entry:

February 27, 1967: "After another tiresome day, marching along the shore and climbing cliffs, we came to the Rosita River . . . We ate our last ration that had been left in reserve, and no signs of life were found in spite of our nearness to the populated areas and the highways."

March 7, 1967: "Four months. The men are becoming more and more discouraged, seeing that we are reaching the end of our supplies, but not the end of the trail. Today we advanced four or five kilometers along the edge of the river and at the end we found a promising path. Food: three and a half birds and the rest of the *palmito*; from tomorrow on, only canned goods, one for every three for two days; then the milk, which is the end."

March 12, 1967: "In an hour and an half we covered the territory opened yesterday. When we arrived, Miguel and Tuma, who had gone ahead, were already exploring in order to try to bypass the steep cliff. The day was spent in this; our only activity was to hunt four little birds which we ate to accompany rice and clams. We have two meals left . . ."

March 16, 1967: "We decided to eat the horse, as our swelling has become alarming. Miguel, Inti, Urbano, Alejandro are presenting various symptoms. I am extremely weak . . ."

Finally, this most unromantic entry: May 13, 1967: "A day of belching, farting, vomiting and diarrhea; a genuine organ concert. We remained in absolute immobility trying to digest the pork. We have two cans of water. I was very sick until I vomited and recuperated . . ."

Characteristic of the revolutionary life, also, are the military virtues demanded of participants: superior will to endure, strict obedience to commands (cooperation), superiority of movement (severely limited, however, by the uncompromising terrain). On June 29th the following: "On the way, I had a conversation with our troop, now composed of 24 men. I pointed out Chino as an example among men; I explained the meaning of the deaths and what the loss of Tuma meant to me personally, whom I considered my own son. I criticized the lack of self-discipline and the slowness of the march and promised to give some basic instructions so that the same thing that happened in the ambush would not happen again, useless losses of life for not obeying rules."

Most revealing, however, in this context, as well as in one entry summing up the characteristics I have distinguished, is the entry for August 3, 1967, which concluded the first nine months of activity, and, at the time, marked the first real low for the movement, which was now reduced, in Che's group, to 22 men, three of whom were crippled, and Che himself burdened by asthma, which he could not stop, for he lacked the simple medicine required, it being confiscated by the enemy. He would soon lose toward the end of August the part of the guerilla which for months he had been trying vainly to contact.

"We walked effectively something like an hour, which seemed more like two to me due to the weariness of the little mare. In a moment of temper, I struck her in the neck with a whip, wounding her badly . . .

"At night I brought everybody together and gave them the following lecture: we are in a difficult situation; Pacho has gotten better today but I am just a human carcass, and the episode of the little mare proves that at some moments I have lost control; that will be modified, but the situation must weigh squarely on everybody and whoever does not feel capable of sustaining it should say so.

"It is one of those moments when great decisions must be take; this type of struggle gives us the opportunity not only to turn ourselves into revolutionaries, the highest level of the human species, but it also allows us to graduate as men; those who cannot reach either one of these two stages should say so and leave the struggle."

Much can be said about this passage, especially the incident of the mare, which bears witness to Che's honesty and integrity, but also puts the question of violence and its effects upon man's character in perspective; I should like to confine myself, however, to the concluding paragraph in which Che addresses his men with what I take to be the essential core of a revolutionary way of life. That is, one is not a revolutionary simply by declaring oneself so and taking up a rifle or placard. No matter how committed one is (and they were at this point nine months and countless privations deep in the guerrilla stage alone), one cannot predicate that term of one-self unless one confronts the next situation in a radical and superior fashion. No matter how may obstacles one has surpassed in the past, it is the next one that matters. It is all or nothing moment by moment. More than that, we must remember that he is telling his men this in one of the darkest hours of the campaign, when success (even survival) appeared impossible. Only in the face of such despair and failure can the true measure of a man be taken, for only then does there exist the opportunity to surpass ourselves, "to turn ourselves into revolutionaries, the highest level of the human species . . . (and it) allows us to graduate as men." The great decision is, then, to continue, to endure in the face of utter defeat: that is revolutionary. To accomplish it is exemplary.

I must take brief note, too, of the fact that he speaks of the revolutionary as the highest level of the human species, not, as Sartre and Fanon do, as the human species, with the consequence that the enemy or oppressor is unhuman or non-human. Che's treatment of prisoners, his relations with his men, and his attitude toward the peasants testifies to his humanity and understanding.

The final characteristic of the revolutionary way of life embraces all the aforementioned ones and gives to the role its dignity and stature: Sacrifice. I think it is evident from the *Diary* that Che did, as Mr. Castro states, sacrifice his own security and hence his life for that of two wounded comrades. And if Mr. Castro's account of his death is accurate, and I have no reason to doubt it, for it is totally consistent with the man, then we must affirm with Ignazio Silone (*Bread and Wine*) that "No word and no gesture can be more persuasive than the life, and, if necessary, the death of a man who strives to be free, loyal, just, sincere, disinterested; a man who shows what a man can be."

Thus this *Diary,* aptly described as being a "revolutionary content, pedagogic, and human," contains within it the characteristics inherent in the revolutionary way of life, violent or non-violent: the isolation of men alone in a struggle against the elements, the apathy of the masses, and the oppressive structures; the intense community life counteracting the isolation, while at the same time sustaining those involved; the totality of the revolutionary thing in so far as the spirit of it must pervade all actions, no matter how minute; the possession and practice of such virtues as endurance, obedience, and movement to a superior degree; the unromantic character of the day by day involvement;

the constant need—better, demand—to surpass oneself even in the face of bitter defeat, and finally, the sacrifice of not only basic needs, but of one's life for the sake of others and the ongoing revolution.

36 EAST FIRST

SEPTEMBER 1968

The most frequent question put to me lately by visitors is, "Well, what do you think of the new house?" and my reply sometimes bewilders them; for the litany of virtues (new, clean, efficient, bright, cheerful, comfortable, secure, well-heated and illuminated) is usually followed by a lament for lost privations (not old, worn, battered with use, besmirched and soiled; nor squalid and foul smelling, insecure and vulnerable, uncomfortable and open to the elements; makeshift and clumsy, dreary and dank). These latter, the marks of indigence, gave an authenticity to our "voluntary" and others' "necessary" poverty.

The neighborhood is different also: the Chrystie Street house was in the (failing) heart of the Bowery, where around the corner were the Round House and the One Mile House; our new house (somewhat removed from the "shopping center" as Ed Brown refers to it) is set amidst a neighborhood of black and Puerto Rican families. The challenges are different here, and so is the atmosphere. Bowery men were at home in the old place; they moved as naturally as deer in a thicket; little was strange there, for the inside of the old house resembled the conditions of their minds and bodies, the streets and the places where they spent their time.

Thus it is not mere nostalgia that makes us think of the old house; rather it was the experience of a community rich in all that is human, while living amid all that was poor.

But even as one dwells on the differences in structure and environment the similarities come crashing in: Fred Lindsey, who came down from the farm for a change of pace, reported this morning, his head and hair still bloodied, that he had his "head caved in" while entering a Bowery hotel last night. And if one closes one's eyes on the first floor of the new house, one cannot really tell there is a difference; for all the sounds and voices are there: Italian Mike's coarse laughter and earthy observations; Scotty's rolling r's, as habitual as his humble request for a quarter; Arthur Sullivan's barking exchanges; Missouri Marie's gentle, high-pitched voice as she offers the *Daily News*; Paul's delight with his cat; and, to answer Dan Kelly's question in a letter from Allenwood Prison Farm, Roger still has his "cheerful smile and his gentle, 'one more guest' attitude when he works the line."

And if one opens one's eyes one finds all the familiar faces and forms in approximately the same places as in the old house: Mary Galligan graciously greeting guests at the door; Bill Harder (sans beard) taking care of his sinks; John McMullen reading the *News* in the corner; Earl Ovitt coming or going from some carpentry job in the basement or backyard; Smokey sitting over his breakfast, always in the same chair at the same table; Milly tidying up after meals; Julie's playful banter with the young people; Polish Walter and Mr.Anderson quietly at the table after their work on the second floor; Walter Kerell with his Harvard Bag filled with mail; Whiskers busy with the donated clothing; Ed Brown's engaging rages and gestures; Wong (called "One Lung" by Italian Mike) silently watching his table as he presses (instead of rolling) a cigarette before waiting on another man.

Much of the furniture—desk, chairs, painting, statues (the statue of our emaciated St.Francis no longer has his back to us, his face to Chrystie Street; now he kneels on a ledge in the front and faces us and our new surroundings), sink and soup oven, kitchen utensils and pots—are all in familiar places; but it is as if some supernatural hand had swept a decade of dirt and grime from the walls and floor where once they were. The fluorescent lights no longer permit shadows to lurk in corners, like some Bowery Man in a doorway. No longer must I dip the roaches from the soup, (later Jack admits to only one or two.-D.D.) where they would fall

from the ceiling of the old house, or idly watch them liberate a
drawer or cupboard. Nor are our nostrils assailed by the sewerage
overflow of the old house ; instead we have the pungent aroma of
soup mixing with the institutionalized odor of disinfectant.

Visitors and Volunteers

Many were the visitors and volunteers during the summer; more,
surely, than I can mention. Tom Temple, Linda Glassner, and Joe
Glossmeyer—all from Oklahoma—were in on much of the moving
from house to house; Janelle Hongess came East for a stay of some
weeks; she fasted with Bob Gilliam, Dan Kelly, and myself,
summers ago in Washington, DC Five young men from Japan have
stayed with us and shared our work. Pat Jordon, a young Franciscan
seminarian, who had to be told to stop working, helped us
exceedingly; especially in his ministrations to Italian Mike, who
refused for a long period to recline completely—he preferred to
sleep sitting up. His condition gradually deteriorated and he was
much in need of the help Pat gave him. The work of caring for him
was continued by our two most recent staff members, Pat May
and Mike Ketchum, who now receive, to their delight, the brunt
of much of Mike's wit. And Mike is better now: the sores on his
legs have healed; he walks by himself now; eats heartily; there is
bite in his cursing, energy in his outbursts, and eloquence in his
gestures (in the Italian manner) as he describes the crease his cane
will put in our heads.

Jonathan Bell and Paul Muller, both young and confronting
the draft, stayed and worked with us and then returned to California
full of plans and hopes. Louise Giovannetti, together with Janelle
and Linda, took up the burden of the evening cooking chores during
the summer. That job has been taken over by Ed Forand, an old
time Catholic Worker, who has returned to us from the world of
gainful employment. Hersha Evans, whose silence is as an ornament,
and Mary Greve, whose sensitivity finds expression in folksong,
are here to spell Ed in the kitchen and help on the paper. Nicole

d'Entremont, Raona Wilson and Nathan are more frequently with us to add their beauty to our lives. Kathy Nackowski and her younger sister visited briefly as they made their way to Salt Lake City from Turkey where they spent the summer. Arthur "The Bishop" Lacey has been with us and assumed the chores of Walter Kerell, who's been on a here-again, gone-again sort of vacation.

Begging

I suggested to Pat May, whose quick intelligence caught the irony in the scene, that we resume our fish-begging thing at the Fulton Street Fish Market. I instructed him briefly in the art, showed him to the cart, and gave him directions to the market, which is quite unlike anything he encountered in Oklahoma. So amongst the stalls of piled fish, cruising cats, and beefy, bare-armed, coarse and earthy fishermen and dealers, he wheeled his cart, crying the CW need, and met with the rude rebuke from some ("That commie bunch!") and from others a silent sort of acceptance. All this time a hard rain fell. He returned sopping wet ("I have no comment at this time," he said) but loaded with perch, striped bass, and full many a large blubbery catfish. He was quite turned on by that scene ("a liberated fishmonger") and it was his thing from then on. That evening, while we were all devouring with relish the results of his begging, we received a phone call from one of the fish deal-ers-the one who had been rude to our man, as he put it, and he had felt rotten all day and wanted to know what kind of fish we wanted. Pat and Mike returned to his stall the next Friday and were offered 300 pounds of salmon, only some thirty pounds of which they could take. Another dealer offered a large tin of fillet, and others contributed more fish. So back they came and we had fish for all the CW people for two days, plus a fish soup for our line; and we still had fish to give to the families on our block with the help of the lady who runs a small grocery store across the street from us. Our many thanks to the men of Fulton Street, who are close to the sea and know what need is.

And at the Hunt's Point Vegetable Market where Mike and Pat beg for vegetables (earlier in the year groups of us picketed those stalls with the Mexican-American and Filipino farm workers) they met with the same rugged generosity, stern warmth, to the point of being invited back the next day when there would be more to take away.

Finally, from Johnny Cash's profoundly human recording of a show recorded at Folsom Prison in California (perhaps only the captured and systematically dehumanized know and respond fully to the human condition) I take a line, "On Monday I was arrested . . ." and apply it to myself. A week ago today, on September 10th, I was arrested by two federal marshals, who came in during the soupline, and taken to Center Street, where I was later indicted for refusal to be indicted into the armed services. Released on my own recognizance, I am to be tried at a yet unknown date in the future.

36 EAST FIRST

NOVEMBER 1968

Winter—bitter, bleak, and ugly—invades New York City as much as the terminal stage of cancer shakes the human body with its pain. Around the morbid growths of the business and industrial areas, colorfully clad citizens scurry to their destinations; the crowds are thicker than in the summer, their pace less leisurely—a mob moving to escape the wind and the cold.

In the outlying areas, the Bowery and Harlem, where the disease has already taken its toll, the sidewalks are deserted except for those without the entrance fee to the sancturaries: that is, fifteen cents or quarter needed to get to a warm bar or $1.25 for a grave-like cubicle in a flop house. In doorways and alleyways, on benches in deserted parks, wrapped in two or three coats or none, these—the unwanted, undestined, unburied—in states of mind and body too blasted to imagine, wait, wait, wait.

More than a dozen flop houses, housing between one and two hundred men each, have closed since last winter. Another ten or so are expected to close within the year. More stringent city building codes, along with the hassle of managing younger men increasingly more hostile, have made the flophouse game unprofitable for the corporations which own them. There is more profit anyway in renting what was once shelter for a hundred men as a loft for two or three artists, as the Lower East Side becomes the East Village. No provision is being made by the city to find shelter for the increasing numbers who will need it. Perhaps the current policy is the city's solution except at Thanksgiving and Christmas, as it has always been: ignore the poor, and perhaps they will wither and fall away.

Our new house is well-heated and the basement room where the Bowery men wait for soup, bread, and tea, is the warmest room in the building. As it gets colder, more men will arrive early, leave late. We feed from a hundred and fifty to two hundred men daily, except during check week, when the line falls off to seventy-five or a hundred. Then everyone gets seconds and thirds on the soups. Fred Lindsey, down from the Farm, has taken over the basement scene during the line. John McMullen and Wong remain our steady waiters, with John sometimes making as well as serving the soup. Bill Harder and Larry pick up on the dishes. Mary Gallagan welcomes the men at the door and directs them to the basement or nearby benches if they're crippled. We know many of the men—some of them remember the CW in three or four of its former locations—but there are many new, and many younger faces on the line, as the drop-outs from the ghettoes across the country, and the new generation of Bowery men, the hippies and yippies, discover that the Great Society has its roots here on the Bowery.

I wonder sometimes what they think of us, as they sit in our kitchen and observe the ways of those who serve them; for the atmosphere is anything but institutional: more along the lines of a wildly incongruous family unabashedly having its squabbles in front of guests.

Preston, who once so diligently took care of the stencils and rolls of addresses of our subscribers, took off one day and has not returned. Gordon McCarthy has reluctantly replaced him at that toil. Italian Mike is alive and well on the second floor, where the focus of the conversation alternates between Mike's bawdy comments to the girls present and Brother John's theological disputes with young volunteers (two of whom, Daniel and Ramond, are from Canada) and cyncial staff members. Arthur Lacey, our hierarchy in residence, is back to help Walter with the backload of paperwork and filing which probably drove Preston away. While Mike

Ketchum went to Oklahoma for Pat Vaught's trial, Pat May supervised the preparationof the October issue for the mails. Now that Mike is back, Pat has left. And so it is with the young people here, whose mobility is not curtailed as is that of the house people.

The Return

Jim Wilson was released from Allenwood Prison Camp and is back with us now. A little thinner, a lot wiser, but very much himself, he's returned to the first floor and works again on the line, or makes soup when Roger or I are not around.

Jim, along with the dozens of other noncooperators in prisons across the country, represents, perhaps, the nonviolent answer to the poignant question posed by the most sensitive and intelligent of young men in our time: "Where can we go? There is no place to go." If what is meant is a meaningful, uncompromised position in our society, then, indeed, there is no place to go. But if what is meant is where can integrity remain intact, conscience unviolated, oppression confronted, then there is always prison, although those recently returned are not eager to encourage anyone to enter it.

I can only admire and applaud the answer given by Alexandros Panaghoulis, convicted of an assassination attempt on Premier Geroge Papadopoulos, to the American-backed Greek regime: "I do not want a stay of execution. I want the execution to be speeded up." The nonviolent equivalent in a society not quite so overtly fascist is prison. Besides, there is really no need in this country for private citizens to get involved in political assassinations, since the Federal government apparently has an agency, adequately financed, willing to perform the necessary tasks.

COGLEY AND THE
RELEVANCE OF RADICALISM

NOVEMBER 1968

I propose to discuss, an article published in the October 30th issue of that most liberal of lay Catholic journals, *The National Catholic Reporter*, entitled "Radical Catholics," (subtitled, "After the Catholic Worker"), by a former Catholic Worker, Mr. John Cogley.

It is Mr. Cogley's thesis that "although radical Catholicism is nothing new to the United States, a radicalized Catholicism is." By the first term, *radical Catholicism*, he refers to the Catholic Worker movement, whose history he traces in broad and generous strokes. By the second term he refers to (I suppose, for he never really tells us) the current issues occupying the minds and energies of the New York (and elsewhere) Catholic Establishment Sophisticates (to borrow a phrase from Daniel Callahan's adjoining article in the same issue) and the hierarchy in various places with which said Sophisticates find themselves embroiled.

"And there is a difference," states Mr. Cogley, between the two forms of radical (or-ized) Catholicism. I would be the first to agree. He goes on to tell us what it is:

It is the difference between those who apply certain sets of beliefs and modes of behavior in their relationship to society and the state but hold back from applying their principles to the church, on the one hand, and, on the other, those who look upon the institutional church as a reflection of the secular society, and therefore a fit target for the same kind of disruption, harassment and critical analysis.

I find I cannot agree with this explanation, for it would appear that the substance of the first term (with the exception of "but hold back from applying their principles to the church") is contained also in the second term; so that the latter group of contemporary radical Catholics appear as some sort of Super Catholic Workers, who have taken on not only the warmongering state, and the affluent Great Society, but the atrophied Roman Catholic Church in America as well.

I'm sure that image is not the one Mr. Cogley wishes to evoke. Or is it?

Again: "disruption, harassment, and critical analysis" are indeed elements of a radical stance; but they are only elements. The radical stance involves a much more basic re-orientation to existing structures, on the one hand, accompanied by a life style which is itself reflective of one's critical analysis in that it affirms what one's analysis denies of the institution to which one is responding. Whether or not the total radical stance is represented by the old radical Catholics or the contemporary radicalizing Catholics is up to each to answer for himself.

The Worker has ever maintained that it is people and not institutions that must be radicalized; it is possible to imagine a totally "radicalized" institution without a single radical in it. We are concerned more with people than with institutions, for we believe that the more concerned people there are, the fewer institutions there will be. (Forgive the Peter Maurinism).

Exception must be taken to Mr. Cogley's exception: that is his phrase, "but hold back from applying their principles to the church." As he himself says elsewhere in the article, the CW "did not hesitate to criticize Cardinal Spellman when he employed seminarians as strikebreakers during the gravediggers strike in 1949; earlier it was bitter about the all out support priests and bishops gave to General Franco during the Spanish Civil War." Nor has it ceased being bitter, nor ceased to criticize the involvement of the

American Catholic Church in the Second World War, Korea, and
Viet Nam. When the young men of the CW choose non-cooperation
with Selective Service and jail, rather than conscientious objection,
whether defined by the State or the American bishops, are they
not applying their principles? Regardless of church or state?

But Mr. Cogley is not denying that the CW holds back on
social policies of ecclesiastical officials when they run counter to
the radical, anarchist, pacifist, pro-union, anti-state principles of
the Worker. He is saying that we do not challenge doctrinal
questions. "To attack," he says, "the idea of the perpetual virginity
of Mary or the notion of the Apostolic Succession in the pages of
the CW would have been looked upon as simply unthinkable."

Rather, really irrelevant. I'm not saying the doctrines are
irrelevant (I'm sure they are relevant to a great many people), but
"to attack" them is irrelevant in the face of war, poverty, starvation,
oppression, and nuclear holocaust. Perhaps it could be said that
such doctrinal questions do not challenge us where we live and
have our being. It is not necessary, after all, to disbelieve in Mary's
virginity in order to make soup, wait on Bowery men, stand in a
picket line; and living as we do in community, we necessarily live
amongst those holding different and opposing beliefs about such
things, and further, reaching the wide spectrum of folk we do who
subscribe to our paper, it would be unkind, in fact unnecessarily
cruel, to point out certain ambiguities in what can only be, on the
part of the individual, a highly personal mode of belief. Would
Mr. Cogley not have us support the farm workers strike because
the Mexican-Americans have an unshakable faith in Our Lady of
Guadalupe? Permit us (if I may speak for CW people) to tilt at our
own windmills. Must we tilt at those of the New York Catholic
Establishment Sophisticates, too? Especially since certain of them
pose no threat to us or our principles?

I wonder what really makes Mr. Cogley wonder that, "What
was remarkable, when one thinks about it, is that so little of this
rebellious spirit was ever turned against the ecclesiastical
establishment." (I wonder also at his sense of time: "was" instead

of "is"—as if the CW were buried somewhere in the radical past of leading Catholic lay liberals). I submit that that rebellious spirit was and is so turned against the establishment that it opted for staying out rather than in it. Far from "holding back from applying its principles to the church," the CW has thrust its principles, its bodies, its houses and farms of hospitality, its monthly minor miracles (given the conditions of life here on the Bowery) in front of the noses of both church and state. The most profound criticism of the ecclesiastical establishment is the very existence of the Catholic Worker—in words and acts, past and present. Moreover, in good Camusian fashion, it says "no" by saying "yes" to unions, blacks, the unalterably poor, peace without victory, communities of service rather than service to self and nation, love—love until it hurts. Mr. Cogley is quite correct when he points out that "Personalism (which might now be translated as 'do your own thing') was the catch-all word used to describe the Worker's emphasis on the role of the individual in society." But he neglected to say that it also describes the role of contemporary Christians (and radicals) in regard to the ecclesiastical establishment. Those early Christian radicals of this century, Dorothy Day and Peter Maurin, went ahead and did their own thing, and those who follow them continue it; but neither were nor are going to wait upon the establishment to catch up to them. There is simply too much to do. Beating dead horses is a waste of energy. Dead men, as Dan Berrigan writes in a recent poem, may be walking in their shrouds; but they're dead, Dan, they're dead.

I do not think that that "special" insight which Mr. Cogley affirms as proper to those new radical Catholics who look upon the "institutional church as a reflection of the secular society" was really missed by the founders or followers of the Catholic Worker movement. It is, after all, rather obvious. But he may be correct in affirming that it is now "a fit target for the same kind of disruption, harassment, and critical analysis." I would prefer the word "fashionable" to "fit" but it does not matter.

What disturbs me also is the attempt on the part of Mr. Cogley (and others who think the Worker is irrelevant) to confine the CW to the Catholic experience in the United States; or, in another way, to deride the CW for not radicalizing the American Catholic establishment. Never was the paper or the movement entitled *the National Catholic Worker* or *American Catholic Worker*. The word Catholic in its title refers with a large "c" to its leadership and with a small "c" to its concerns and, thankfully, to its appeal. The religious concerns of the Worker, for example, embrace both of James' distinctions within the religious field, that of the institutional, with its emphasis on mass and ceremony, and that of the personal religious experience, with its emphasis on conscience and incompleteness, need for community and sacrifice. If the person of the Pope, as Mr. Cogley says, was treated as sacrosanct, it is true to say also that the person of Roger LaPorte was treated as sacrosanct.

The contemporary Catholic radicals whom Mr. Cogley defends and represents may, if they wish, attempt to radicalize the American Catholic establishment. I really cannot get excited about such a thing, and am tempted to think it irrelevant . A dead horse on its feet is still a dead horse. We are simply Catholic Workers, not Professional Catholics.

It is with reluctance that I approach Mr. Cogley's conclusion, for, in tone and substance, it epitomizes the liberal view. I quote it in full and conclude:

The difference between Dorothy Day and the contemporary Catholic radicals, I suppose, is rooted in a changed theology. In the old days, the notion of the church as a divine institution over-shadowed its human aspects. Today, the opposite may be more true. The proper balance, if there is such a thing, remains to be achieved.

Granting my bias, I am inclined to affirm (paraphrasing Etienne Gilson) that new radicalism can no more replace old radicalism than new truths replace old truths. The best that new truths can do is replace old errors. The truths expounded by the CW, and I defy anyone in the post-Pope John period to deny them, are not the CW's. They belong, in fact, to the church: that is to that tradition coeval-with-the-institutional-church of enthusiastic Christianity, which has ever lived face to face with the parousia and consequently, lived out its ethic in the here and now with Franciscan abandon, as Mr. Cogley puts it. The old and the new radicalism, do not, no more than the new theology, seek new truths; rather all, if they be truly radical and bent on the root of being, search for the old truths hidden behind the tapestries and travesties of time. There, in the barren darkness, they approach the shadowed, huddled figures by the fire and hear those voices in unison calling to them: "Peace, Brother. Come, join us by the fire. Share our food. To hell with the arrogance of the chieftains!"

36 EAST FIRST STREET

DECEMBER 1968

To Dan Kelly
Allenwood Prison Farm
Allenwood, Pennsylvania

Dear Dan:

Remember the classic *faux pas* I made when last I used this column as a private-public letter to Jim Wilson, who was then where you are now: in Allenwood Prison? I addressed him in the salutation as "Dead Jim," not "Dear Jim"; and to this day we do not know whether the original error was in my copy (which is missing) or simply a fantastic fluke on the part of the printer.

Perhaps, overzealous in my effort to identify with Jim in prison, I subconsciously gave a name to his state of mind at the time. I hope and trust that it is not your state of mind. I prefer to regard such events as that painfully poignant salutation as metaphysical mysteries and leave it at that. A week or so ago, shortly before 10 o'clock when we serve our soup, bread, and tea, it was discovered that we had no tea.

Being short of help that day, we could not send anyone out for some, so we reluctantly took the cups from the tables. At that moment the nuns who regularly donate bread and cake to us arrived, and, you guessed it, in one of the cartons was a pound and a half of excellant tea.

And our soupline let it be said, as I still maintain about the old Latin Mass, that it is a work of art from beginning to end. There is something of the artist (as Pat May says) in John McMullen, who now is in charge of the soup thing, as he orchestrates pandemonium every morning to an appreciative audience. To those too timid to ask for seconds, he says: "Let me put a head on that bowl of soup." Wong, stern and brusque, is effective counterpoint, and Fred Lindsey takes up the theme downstairs, where he entertains the troops with his burlesque rountines.

There are other themes, of course: Louis Prinz, who along with Italian Mike, Brother John, Jimmy the Indian, and others, regularly works on the second floor, told me he knows more than a few Bowery men who come in not for soup alone but to meditate in those intervals of silence following raucous discord. And the curtain rises and falls on the lilting greeting and farewell of our Scottish Mary Gallagan.

Of Prisoners

I am rather glad, I must admit, that my sentencing and time (mid-January; probably at Allenwood) postdate the upcoming "action" on the part of the ambitious Peace Movement at Allenwood on the 20th of December. I understand it is to be another "celebration of life" thing, complete with Joan Baez and Freedom songs.

Besides making prison officals uptight, the probable consequence more rigid routines, there are other objections. I would delight, were I in prison, to be sung to and made to feel good; but I would be depressed as hell, were I in prison, to be singled out, sung to, and made to feel holy.

So blessed, how would I face this other guy (or he, me) who's in for unhallowed bootlegging (there's freedom for you; anarchy, too)?

I would not have any fellow-prisoner put in Prufrock's position: "I have heard the mermaids singing, each to each. I do not think that they will sing to me." The beauty and profoundity of Johnny Cash's performance at Folsom Prison resides in his singing to all the prisoners as prisoners. And affirming them and what they think and how they feel, to boot. "They are all my brothers," he states on the record jacket. He wasn't speaking about "political prisoners" then, but of the addicts, the murderers, the rapists—all of them—who were not only his audience but the subjects of his songs. Dostoyevsky somewhere in The Brothers Karamazov wrote: "No one can judge a criminal, until he recognizes that he is just such a criminal as the man standing before him, and that he perhaps is more than all men to blame for that crime."

I frankly don't believe in "political prisoners"; or, rather, I believe all prisoners are "political prisoners." Their "tactics" may differ from the Peace Movement's, but they're up against the same damned structure. What makes the repressive and unjust laws that put peace people behind bars any more repressive and unjust (hence, worthy of extraordinary protest) than those that put others behind bars? The politically minded, outraged at injustices wrought upon minority groups, the poor, and the war-wracked, are they to be singled out and set apart from the people for whom they struggled?

You write of the "annual Christmas card deluge" that descends (unlike the gentle rain) only on the heads of political prisoners. You say "a disconcerting number of senders use a sticker or stamp for their own address." Well, we know what prison they're in. Shaw wrote: 'Whilst we have prisons it matters little which of us occupies the cells."

On Sabotage

You write that Mike Ketchum's article about the Catonsville action "almost moved me to the drastic action of writing a rebuttal. Is it possible that he does not see the witness and call to conscience" inherent in that event? No, it is not possilbe that such a witness be unacknowledged. No one denies the witness and the call to conscience. On that level of nonviolent action, the Catonsville response was beautiful and eloquent. But when the action is touted about as "The burning of the Catonsville fires signals a shift in tactics, from nonviolent protest to resistence to revolution," as Tom Cornell put it, I, for one, must disagree.

Three errors, I submit, permeate Cornell's contention: first, a misunderstanding of the nature of the nonviolent revolution (not to be dismissed as simply protest and picketing); second, the misguided attempt to keep in step with the violent "guerilla" movement (not a revolution) now in vogue; third, misconstructing a tangental action for an essential "shift in tactics" or a "new stage" in the nonviolent thing.

To take the last first: When zealous sympathizers of Cesar Chavez' nonviolent farmworkers union burn down packing sheds belonging to the fat-cat grower, or, as in Rio Grande City, burn down a railroad trestle so that struck produce cannot leave the area, these actions, fully understood by Chavez, are not union policy, even though they represent, perhaps, the state of mind of many of the rank and file. Even though such actions are directed against material as opposed to human objects, the union must refuse to sanction them, for they are, in fact, violent. During the past summer, we here at the Worker had occasion, being free, bustible, and nonunion, to engage in what we jokingly referred to as nonviolent sabotage of certain chain stores selling California grapes. Slight property damage (in the form of squashed fruits, etc. on the bottom of heavily packed carts left unpaid for in protest) and expense in terms of employee wages for time spent repacking goods, together with the bad image in the eyes of the consumer left by hassle between evil manager vs. farmworker-defenders, were the results of such action. The union will not rise or fall upon it. But at a certain point such action had a place; if not in union policy, at least in the consciences of its sympathizers.

So, too, on a larger, more consequential level, the Milwaukee and Catonsville actions.

Concerning the second error, the obvious need not be argued. Concerning the first, I, presumptuously perhaps, refer to my article on Che Guevara's *Diary*, (July-August CW) which is a thinly disguised analysis of the characteristics of both violent and non-violent revolutions.

On Weddings

There will be two. On December 30 Nicole d'Entremont and Michael Ketchum will be wed. Their ceremony to take place at Most Holy Crucifix Church, Broome Street, Manhattan. The reception to be held here at the Worker. On January 4 Hersha Evans and myself will wed. The ceremony and reception to be held here in the soup kitchen. Father Dan Berrigan will join us. Come, share our joy.

JAILED EDITORS WRITE

FEBRUARY 1969

The following letters were received last month from two of our associate editors who are serving penitentiary sentences for refusing to take part in the bloodletting in Viet Nam or cooperate with the Selective Service system. Jack Cook's letter was written from the Federal House of Detention in New York City; he has since joined former CW staff Dave Miller and Dan Kelly at the Allenwood (Pennsylvania) Federal prison. Bob Gilliam is incarcerated at Sandstone prison in Minnesota.

January 18th

Dear Walter and Family:

If I have written enough "Chrystie Streets" to fill some circular file, I find myself delighted now with the idea of writing *to* everyone instead of about everyone.

For the first two days, I had to smoke Bugler in my pipe and now sympathize with everyone (especially Smokey Joe) who is confined to them. (Pass those packaged butts around more freely, Walter; go get a job and support the cigarette bill or sell some of your art work.) Later, a black and a Puerto Rican provided me with pipe tobacco until the commissary opened and I bought some and paid back my debts.

Thank Earl Ovitt for coming to the sentencing and apologize to Mary Galligan, John McMullen, Ed Brown, and Fred Lindsey for my not saying anything before I left—

I was about to burst out crying, just as Nathan Wilson used to when Raona left the room.

I miss everyone.

The soup here, John, is always bean (or so far at least) and that's it—bean; not much meat in it. As a protest, I take the tin soup bowl but use it for coffee instead. There is plenty to eat and you're not rushed if you time it right. I'm going to try to lose this gut that I acquired on the Bowery; since they don't sell ale here I've got a good chance. The food isn't bad either, for the cooks are professional guys in trouble. Because I write and can use the language they assigned me to the Captain's office as clerk-announcer; one of the blacks in my cell block is a professional cook from upstate, so he is now in the kitchen.

They made me shave my mustache off, so I now look a little like Whiskers a while ago. I'm growing it back again, though. I think I got more exercise at First Street than I do now; I'm not running anywhere, just pacing fourteen steps one way and back again. I'll soon be as good at it as Famine, maybe.

Sorry I didn't see Tony before I left to thank him again and again for setting up that marriage reception for Hersha and me. I hope Pat May is not being harassed or burdened with too much of the thing since I left. Ed Forand, too. Give Italian Mike a can of beer for me, and to all there—including Paul—my love and warmest wishes.

I haven't seen the sky for days now, but I hope it's fair and that the sun shines on all of you.

Love,

Jack

WHO WAS THERE WHEN YOU DIED?

(for Missouri Marie; age unknown;

relatives unfound)

APRIL 1969

Who was there when you died?
No, none of us who knew you were.
Far from the port all sailors know
You wrecked, at last, in sanitary seas.

Dorothy visited that afternoon,
You wept and prayed and spoke
Of Job and how courage comes;
Tiers of Cardinals could not contain
What of God transpired there.

Efficient faces with rehearsed fondness
Gave odd names to pain, a constant friend,
Insisted on surgery,
Dismissed your only weapon, prayer.

To claims of hygiene and health,
Ours and theirs,
Face tightened against pain, (as once
Knarled hands clasped the broom
And taught the mute instrument to move)
You yielded,
Meek and humble as a gift,
To a weaker gave the chore,
And delivered up your body,
(So with yesterday's *Daily News* you bore
Good News to those who love folly)
And sank under unfamiliar sheets, (you
Who kept night's vigil in a hardback chair
And watched dawn unshroud shadows once more).

Unacquainted with impersonal civil plenty
And the company of those newly come to Death's door,
You longed for your threadbare wool hat
That you said would shed all rain,
Two faded dresses, unashamed pin,
Shopping bags filled with discarded wares,
The tools of your art,
Now beyond reach of your hand.

You longed to return to the Bowery,
Little Italy and Second Avenue to Eighth Street,
Among the lost and outcast
You shared streets and handouts
Vacant lots, encrusted tenements were home.

You once told David Susskind,
Who laughed behind his hand,
As he entertained the masses,
With misery and shame,
That there was no tinsel on the Bowery,
Nor, may I add, makeup for the mind.

From your kin in wit, way, and burden
You were taken,
O, all the emblems of your state
They seized and burned:

But your soul, alone in the white sea,
Faceless in their poverty,
In misery without a name,
Before the knives touched faith,
Heard the stillness in the whirlwind
And from good intentions begged your fame.

THREE PRISON POEMS

MAY 1969

WAYS OF DOING TIME

Cry, detecting eye,
Warning of the pupil—
Drown, caged clamor,
In stilled hiatus of "why?"

Learn, pinioned man,
The rule you teach so well:
Solitude is the answer
Cursed consequences span.

Distraction is the game's name,
Thought lost to a full hand.
Once again royalty's debtor
Wallows in dubious fame.

Clubs and spades parade our days,
Cardboard caught in the lie,
Loss whispers down the well,
We bid the evening good-bye.

Refurbished memories are sweet,
Orgies of the mind,
Waste of will is a flesh filter
Seek the cave where two springs meet.

Fantasies wedge the wedded apart,
Sex for the other in each is spent;
But the two-souled river winds
About the island with selfless art.

Let inane arguments reverberate,
Mouth to mouth you mock the eye,
Stone walls will be useful then,
Prisoners alone lock the gate.

Tell us again what the judge did,
How lawyers fail and friends part,
Redream the agony again, again,
A year tomorrow is also dead.

Lift that iron, that weight of anger,
Curse the battler, cry down the weak,
Win or lose, it's never too late,
Compete for the laurel of murder.

Old prisoners jog to Death's gate
The young to keep a dream awake;
But a body in prison is not aware
That he's unhinged and fighting fate.

TO MY WIFE

The liberal types
from California
asked you
"What do you think this sentence will do
to the relationship you and Jack share?"
Briefly you answered
(Silently noting how
comfortably they sat)
a soft word escaped you

a child is born unto us

Into that naked soupkitchen
students of hunger and need
play sadly the game of survival
by gutters strewn with a moment's release
the bottle broken and the headless toy
on benches and crawling chairs
spitted coat, urine-black crotch
wipers wash the stench from the eyes
men bent on a home away
from the wrecked bodies of cars and men
In a house awaiting its next death
a wall-less, wardenless, wordless prison
drink finally has made it work
though Bowery down they are minds away
life complains in drowning cells
ease has departed the stricken city
pain stalks in every part
muscles no longer master a move
the near dead and wounded tear
at the health of a passerby,
infect the strong, take the crutch from the weak

so all might meet at the black edge
equal, alone, and naked

a child is born unto us

Into this mean lit corridor.
nobody's unhigh anyschool
unengaged charade of suburbia
by pastel bunk and locker
"One sheet and a pillowcase only"
Two Army blankets and a meal sack
near a john with super-flush toilets
Lane of lovelorn after dark
water fountains turned frigidaire
to the march of dominoes' clock
the din of perpetual TV
shiny-clap-heel-clop of shower pads
word wargames of Puerto Ricans
Black slang's dark caress
Time turns the mute ear
unargued, unidled it stays
near sockets plugged with stringers
instant coffee at a buzzing coil
wild heart at mail call
count, then, a chamber filled with curses
wrath's back, rage smothered in a mask
bootcamp without sargeants
all pretenders to the role
red face from a PA box
O coarse bourgeoisie cloister
your silence and rule are not mine

a child is born unto us

They asked, "Do you ever feel frustrated?"

A gentle rain awakens my face
where drops fall light breaks;
day's disparate elements brace
as your image my mind makes

delicate branches brimmed with dew
in symmetry so clean and bright;
gently my thoughts cover you
as limbs in mist soar in the light

a child is born

Though we abide in separate prisons
Our day's shattered by recurring pain;
Need knows no special seasons,
Alone love forges our chain

Such suffering wed on a whirling anvil
Amid chaos, war, and pain gone wild;
Everywhere lay the victims of overkill—
Despair, darkness, at the spark of a child.

Prayer

Were I to state my emotional pitch,
As I stand here by my metal locker,
Upon the top of which I lean and write,
To wring a bit of concentrated sense,
Out of this trafficked corridor's havoc,
Trembling, I vibrate somewhere between
Conscientious objectors plunking dull guitars

And the concatenation of angry dominoes.
But I cannot castigate the way men do their time,
Faced with myth, deceit, and murder, the young discover song.
Emerging from bitter places, others embrace waste.
May I, caught in space and time, interpolate with grace.

POST-PRISON POEMS

FEBRUARY 1971

Soupline Revisited

As if two years ago today
(We meet again outside the Worker)
Were but a prolonged yesterday,
He and Blacky, his still sole partner,
Forget the cold and downward way.
"Hi, Man," "You've been gone a bit," he signs.
My hand reaches out in warmth and play—
But strange scene! Our eyes suddenly die—
To see, to touch where lost fingers cry.

In Deerfield, Massachusetts

For Tricia and David

I celebrate the gentle ways
Your snowbound quiet home affords;
This little house so richly filled
With all that is needed, ennobled, and loved;
My tension-twisted First Street soul
Unwinds, and, as the drifted byway
Smoothed by the noxious snow-mobile,
My churning mind now softly rolls
In easy rhythm through dark and day.

David, we are miles, we are miles
From the prison life we shared;
Yet as Ahab felt still his lost leg,
So we, too, though free, remain barred—
From the common pursuits, the ruts, and files
Upon files of those who ingenuously beg
Accomplishment, as in iron cradles they climb
A weekend mountain; then wind down—sleek pegs
Seeking refuge in safe and sanitary holes.

O, Gentle ones, stay loved and loving still.

JOHN DUNN HUNTER:
VICTIM AND MEASURE

SEPTEMBER 1973

"There is no human being on earth capable of declaring with certitude who he is. No one knows what he has come into the world to do, what his acts correspond to, his sentiments, his ideas, or what his real name is . . . History is an immense liturgical text where the iota's and the dots are worth no less than the entire verses or chapters, but the importance of one and the other is indeterminable and profoundly hidden." -Leon Bloy

My friend, Dick Drinnon, and I have argued often in the past about the role of history and religion in our lives. I recall distinctly, as an inmate in Allenwood Federal Prison, receiving from him the phrase "impeccable rectitude" in response to, I'm sure, my overtly righteous scribbling about teachers still enjoying, as I was not, the amenities of the academic life. But I got even. I was there two years later with that phrase the day he was subpoenaed to appear before the Grand Jury during the early stages of the Harrisburg Trial. So it is with some glee that I open this review of his work *White Savage: The Case of John Dunn Hunter* with Bloy's definition of history as an "immense liturgical text." I can see Dick glower. Bellow away, my friend, you cannot squirm out of it. It is as if Bloy was himself commenting on John Dunn Hunter, on your book, on you. More, you and your book clarify and concretize Bloy's mystical "history." In the "expansive destiny of the United States," to use Drinnon's phrase, John Dunn Hunter is an "iota." In the official version of the Winning of the West he was made into an "ellipsis." One may legitimately ask why a major historian, author of the definitive biography of Emma Goldman, *Rebel in Paradise*, should concern himself with a totally unknown man, who did not even know his own name, who was taken captive by Indians at the age of two or three in 1799 or 1800; who in the Who's Who of What's What is not; who though he wrote a book about the manners and customs of Indians and an account of his captivity, and achieved his period's instant fame, lionized here and abroad, was totally forgotten by successive generations, even those concerned with rekindling the myth of the Wild West; who, though he knew Jefferson, Robert Owen, and many other influential men, was labeled a fraud and an impostor by the then leading expert on Indian affairs, Lewis Cass, and has remained such in professional opinion until now; who was assassinated at the instigation of American officials after having unsuccessfully tried to unite red and white men together in the Republic of Fredonia.

Symbol of America

The question is legitimate. The answer is found in Bloy. Or one answer anyway. John Dunn Hunter was a victim. We, as Americans, are trained to kneel at the Shrine of Success, which dates back to our Constitution and the Founding Fathers. It is truer, I submit, to take the measure of our achievement as a people by studying our victims. Some insight into our national character, the better aspects, the redeeming qualities that is, are best revealed in a study, not of ourselves as victors, but as victims of that Revolution. Victims. Moral Hermaphrodites. That term, startling as it is, best defines Hunter and a host of others who contain within themselves the dual tensions of creativity and receptivity that set them apart from, and frequently in opposition to, the rest of humankind. That the term "moral hermaphrodite," use by Balzac (probably thinking of himself as well) in reference to Cooper's Leatherstocking, and applied by Drinnon to Hunter in the excellent Epilogue of this work, is synonymous, I do believe, with "victim," will be apparent once the term "savage" is stripped of its acquired characteristics, to stand revealed as referring to a pristine, one-on-one, thoroughly honest relationship of the individual to his conscience, to his need to be at one with his being and with Nature, to his yearning to be free of the fetters of man-made laws, to be in essential opposition to state-imposed pain. The "host" I speak of, as Bloy contended, the dots and iota's of misfortune, spans time and space. Not for nothing did I hesitate to write this piece until the day the Indians surrendered their weapons at Wounded Knee. The attempt to make Hunter, his sentiments, his ideas, his very name into an ellipsis, has failed. With this work, we are confronted by the unique challenge he put to his time. As Drinnon puts it:John Dunn Hunter came forward to challenge the myth that the United States government was the primary engine of a beneficent Progress. Not by accident was he opposed and put down by two men who became Secretaries of War and by a third who colonized a state. He was first the victim of character assassination and then of physical assassination because he dared to speak and act for the Indians. And the attack on him, of course, was merely an incident in the Three Hundred Years' War against the red man (p.245). And Drinnon himself comes forward to challenge the perennial myths of the dominant school of American history, represented by such respected men as Henry Steel Commager, who, as lately as a recent issue of *The New York Review of Books* (19 July 1973) looks with horror at the current scandals of Watergate and posits a dismal change in the American character which once was so nobly represented by Jefferson, Washington, etc., who knew, according to his view, that "virtue is the animating principle of a republic. And to the Commonwealth they served—almost always at great personal sacrifice—they paid the tribute of virtue."

Victim's Victory

Drinnon guides us through the "great gap between Jefferson's words and his deeds," and we in turn reach the dismal conclusion that the national character has not really changed—the political rhetoric is simply of a lower quality. Jefferson could say grandly: "Humanity enjoins us to teach them agriculture and the domestic arts" in his second Inaugural Address, but in private papers, corresponding to his "removal policy," he wished to obtain from the "native proprietors the whole left bank of the Mississippi." As Drinnon states, Jefferson acquired "some one hundred million acres in treaties shot through with fraud, bribery, and intimidation. And when Indians interfered with national interest, as did the 'backward' tribes of the Northwest in 1812, Jefferson's humanitarianism hardened: 'These will relapse into barbarism and misery, lose numbers by war and want,' he grimly predicted to John Adams, 'and we shall be obliged to drive them, with the beasts of the forests into the Stony mountains.'" (page 157). Again, concerning racism and Jefferson, Drinnon writes:From the point of view of citizens of the United States, it had long been recognized that blacks could except no room at the inn or anywhere else in what would be a ' White Man's Country.' Shortly after the turn of the century, President Jefferson had written James Monroe then Governor of Virginia, his rhapsodic reflections on a destiny that was manifestly white: Americans would multiply and 'cover the whole northern if not southern continent, with a people speaking the same language, governed in similar forms, and by similar laws; nor can we contemplate with satisfaction either blot or mixture on that surface' (page 169-170). But revisionist history is not concerned primarily, as its detractors argue, with debunking national figures. Drinnon did not write a biography of Jefferson; he wrote a biography of a *dot*. Of a leader who was not permitted to lead; of a man of stature who was not permitted to stand; of a victim whose victory was real—in the spiritual sphere at least. Perhaps it is in that sphere alone that America has met its challenges. We needn't posit

the advanced, liberated consciences of our day and say some at
least have come to grips with the American nightmare. At its very
origins this country produced men of vision (Hunter was one,
George Catlin another) who had solved the problems of uniting
the variegated tensions—white, black, and red—that wrap like
bandages around our body politic. But these men were not permitted to live and work in peace.

The Reality Underneath

Nor is revisionist history concerned with "if this had happened" or
"if he had lived." It is not visionary. It is concerned with alternative courses of action in the present, based on alternative interpretations of events and people in the past. It is a living history. It
does not attempt to substitute one set of myths for another: it
does attempt to see through various myths to the reality under-
neath. If entire verses and chapters of American history read more
like a Mickey Spillane novel (as Drinnon will argue) than the liturgical text Bloy posited, revisionist history teaches us that,
throughout this period, there were those who lived and died—
and not simply rhetorically or patently historically—for noble
causes. Victims, if you will. The dots and iota's. They have uncom-
mon anonymity. Some, infamy. Such as John Brown. But the dots
are connected. Another such man, whose name is famous but whose
wisdom is officially infamous, is Henry David Thoreau, Thoreau
read Hunter's book and Cass's attacks on him; he copied some
thirty-seven pages in all of Hunter's narrative in his Indian Note-
books, and, as Drinnon states, he "must have winced while copy-
ing out Cass's assertion that the narrative was 'a useless
publication.'"When Thoreau wrote of 'wild men, so much more
like ourselves than they are unlike,' he revealed an ongoing process
of redefinition which only his death cut short—his last words were
said to have been 'moose' and 'Indian.' Thoreau was redefining
civilization and savagery, terms badly in need of redefinition then
and so desperately needed today . . . To say that wild men were

fundamentally like ourselves was to announce a radical break from the consensus of Cass and most white Americans. Like other former colonials, the people of the United States had established a society in which non-Europeans were nonpeople. Everywhere the native was subjugated or slaughtered, or he was culturally castrated and herded onto reservations. The pattern in the United State had its own configurations, however, based mainly on the distance between its doctrines of universal Christian brotherhood and of Enlightenment natural rights, on the one hand, and its practice of Indian removal or extermination, on the other (page 250). Again: Thoreau may easily have seen in Hunter, with his hauntingly allegorical name, a symbol of the meaning of America. Out of the encounter of the Old World with the New, white with red, was born a new man who sought a new heaven and a new earth where extermination was not one of the standing orders of providence. A new man no longer at war with the nature in himself or engaged in a frenzy of conquest of the nature without (page 252). As Drinnon states, it was sad beyond words that Thoreau did not live to write his masterpiece on the Indians. But it is a joy that Drinnon has done what Thoreau's death left undone. The immense liturgical text has been significantly illuminated. Illuminated by one for whom, as Emerson said of Thoreau, "Every fact lay in glory in his mind."

THE MONUMENT

JUNE-JULY 1983

Despite the cold and a high wind, the joggers were out in force. At noon, on the mall approaching Lincoln's Memorial, walkers be wary. Old Abe from his great height commands, but now is not the time to meditate, as wave after wave of the hardy, the overweight, the trendy—in sum, the hurried representatives of each of Erikson's identity crises jog by. A mere walker feels pelted. Atomized?

But there we were—Ellen, our one-year-old daughter Cynthia, and I—on our way to see the Vietnam Memorial. I had been told by card-playing park attendants in their truck at the base of the Washington Monument that it was "to the right of the Lincoln Memorial." As the window closed on that information and I turned away, only the fierce wind seemed out of the ordinary. It was difficult to imagine that night, a few weeks ago when, in O'Hara's bar, Main Street, Owego, I had watched on the tube this very spot as the hapless, bombless anti-nuclear protester—our generation's "Weird John Brown"—drove to his final act.

In her stroller, Cynthia doubled over in an effort to escape the wind. We released her. Bundled under Ellen's poncho, she was soon asleep as we walked amid the streaming joggers. A path to the right distracted me from the cabin-born rail-splitter now encased in gothic glory, and soon we had our first glimpse of the Viet Nam Memorial. We looked down to see it.

The contrast was striking. Head lifted, eyes skyward, my neck soon felt the strain of looking up at Lincoln. Head bowed, my

body lunged down the slope to what appeared to be some monstrous cavern opening. One man—in proportion, an Americanized Jehovah—at the top of the knoll; at its foot, over fifty-eight
thousand sandblasted names stuck in the mud. Beyond Lincoln
there was only sky; beyond the names in the shiny black marble
was my own reflection. Lincoln's marble steps wear well. The
mourners at the wall have chewed the lawn approaching it to pieces.
I have seen a pasture wherein a herd of cows, newly separated from
their calves, have so churned the ground in circuit of the fence that
they marched in mourning knee-deep in mud, the black stain of
their weeping ran inch-wide down their faces. So was the space
before the black marble memorial. A four-foot wide deck was set
in place and humbly ran its length. a plain wooden table at one
end held literature about MIA's. Three long-haired vets in battle
fatigues, high on grief and their staggering roles, stood guard, I
longed to stop and talk; but the baby, the cold, the long walk back
forbade it.

Ellen asked one of the two attendants, who, book in hand,
stood near the center of the memorial, about an Owego boy, a
friend of her brother. His name was duly found a short way off in
the middle of a black slab, surrounded by other names, even that
of a namesake of mine. It was weird.

One face to which I could not put a name kept recurring to
my mind. He was a Lt.Col. in charge of ROTC at Hobart College
in the mid-sixties. I was an instructor in English at Hobart then,
and for the two years prior had been counseling students faced
with the draft. My essential occupation deferment became too
heavy to carry, so I sent my draft cards back, quit academe, and
joined the Peace Movement. Shortly afterwards, the Lt.Col. resigned his post and took up active duty in Viet Nam. In New York
City, an associate editor of *The Catholic Worker*, I was organizing
the first Non-cooperators Against the Draft Conference in the fall
of 1967 when I learned of his death. Shot down over Viet Nam.
Students at Hobart did not lack examples. His name was in that

marble, somewhere. He took his job seriously. I honor him but especially as a teacher do I remember him.

Other faces occurred to me: some had fought and died, others served only to come home to scorn. And the faces of AWOL soldiers whom we housed and then put on the next leg of their underground trip to Canada. Or the faces of the young men struggling with Conscientious Objector forms, their families' fears, and their own inchoate opposition to the war. I remembered, too, the faces of my students who fled to Canada; those who wiped themselves out with drugs; others who became COs or, joining the Guard, summer soldiers. And then I remembered those who chose federal prison rather than war, only to find both. Two of the seven years that I engaged in anti-war activity were spent in federal prisons. I heard the lowing of those mourning cows from inside the education building of the Allenwood Federal Prison Camp, where I and other prisoners held class.

The victims of the war at home have no monument, nor do the hundreds of thousands of Vietnamese. Yet that monstrous cavern opening seemed to beckon to us all.

But I would not have it so. From beneath the poncho, Cynthia's tiny hand stretched forth to find her mother's ear. We moved away. Looking back, the ever-diminishing black monument resembled some cosmic boomerang, snatched out of time and space, and stuck forever in the earth. Not quite buried, (though official Washington would prefer it so), as the war can never be quite forgotten. The recurrent nightmares, the effects of Agent Orange, veteran unemployment and suicide, the massive resistance to registration, the government's attempt to bury conscientious objection status— El Salvador—all attest to the war's recurring effects. There is no escape. A boomerang. Seeing it there in all its awesome blackness, I longed to place my head against it. Not to still its movement— I could not, no more than I could stop the war—but to still mine.

THE FACE OF FALSEHOOD

MARCH 1987

(The following is excerpted from the preface of Jack Cook's recent book, *The Face of Falsehood, the Key to Moby-Dick and Mosses From an Old Manse,* **published by Anthoensen Press. It is available c/o PO Box 474, Owego, NY 13827. Eds. note).**

Not long out of prison, and with my prison books behind me, I wanted to write about [Melville]; for he had helped me to do time in prison. Between counts, before and after mess-lines, I poured over the Hendricks House edition of his collected poems, especially *Battle-Pieces and Aspects of the War.* I lived for months within minutes on the *Pequod* or in the South Seas with *Typee* and *Omoo.* To live that way in prison is to do good time as opposed to bad time. For reading is a way of survival in prison. Other authors helped me, too: Hawthorne, Shakespeare, Kazantzakis. But Melville more than others. Frost, Hemingway, Updike, and assorted others were of no help to me. I did not analyze the books that did not work. I rejected them. Now I think I have some understanding of why some authors worked and others did not; but then it was a matter of need. The need to escape.

It was not simply a matter of escaping into fantasy. If that were the case, a mere western would do for me as it does for many prisoners. I needed to escape from the state of mind, the state of being, of a prisoner. For a prisoner—powerless and unable to do or perform, for that is the will of those who imprison—to remain a prisoner in mind as well as body, is ultimately to imprison oneself. No matter if one is a political prisoner or a bank robber, the uniforms are the same and the state of mind and spirit created by the conditions might well be the same if one did not escape. Reading was my escape into meaning.

But there are times in prison when one cannot read. In solitary one is deprived of books, friends, tobacco, even toothpaste. At times, even water to drink. In solitary they try to deprive one of all human contact. One is reduced to a caged animal; the only approved contact is the cage keeper. I did several stints in solitary as punishment for political actions within the prison, including attempted escape. But the best laid plans of prison officials, as prison literature from Socrates on testifies, often go awry.

The Human Condition Anew

Sitting or pacing, naked and alone, in my strip cell at Lewisburg Penitentiary, during the hottest August I can recall, I peopled my cell with a crowd of friends, family, lovers, artists, ancestors, and enemies, large and small, I have written of that immediate experience in my *Rags of Time: A Season in Prison* (Beacon, 1972). Deprived of human companionship as most of us know it, I created the human condition anew. Melville and Hawthorne were there, of course. My green mattress in the center of the cell floor was an island in the South Seas or Morton's Merry Mount. Had not Melville been in a prison of sorts for mutiny, which is still the prison word for escape? Had not Hawthorne joined, for a year, a radical community of worker-scholars? Had not Melville walked the Bowery long before I did? Was not the Bowery still, and the Catholic Worker House of Hospitality since the thirties', the last refuge for mariners, outcasts, and castaways? Did not my ancestors live around the corner from the Hawthorns of Salem in 1650? Wasn't John Cook, one of the accusers during the Salem witch trials, an ancestor?

I welcomed them all into my cell. I know that, in speaking of one's ancestors, one speaks of other people; yet at no time have they seemed so important as in a strip cell. When the hack growled, "Cook, in here!" I entered, it seemed, with my ancestors on either side.

William and Jediciah were there: Revolutionary son and Tory father. From age fourteen, William served in the first Connecticut regiment, 1777 to 1783; later he became a doctor in Durham, New York. According to the *History of Green County, New York* (Beers, 1984) he was with Washington in Morristown, New Jersey, during the winter of 1777-1778, and left this: "Washington used to come round and look into our tents, and he looked so kind, and he said so tenderly, 'Men, can you bear it?' 'Yes, General, yes, we can,' was the reply, 'and if you wish us to act, give us the word and we are ready.'" William's father, whose grandfather helped found Wallingford, fled to New Brunswick, Canada, and, when he died, left William five shillings, shades of Hawthorn's Robin and the Old Tory. They were good company for an American non-combatant of the 1960s. I felt as if I were rounding out their original experience of empire building.

We were joined by William's son, George and his grandson, William Morris. George, according to the family Bible, at age twenty-nine fell on the morning of the 25th of March 1829 from the Spanker beam of the ship Hamilton on her passage from Liverpool to New York and drowned. Thomas Morris wrote for William Bennett's *New York Herald:* he covered Farragaut's victory at Mobile, the bombardment of Fort Fisher, and the Battles of Chancellorville and Gettysburg. According to tradition, he quarreled with Bennett after his Gettysburg dispatch and was fired; his article appears under a different by-line in a later edition. But still later, at Bennett's request, he is in San Francisco to start up a newspaper there. I knew little more of these men and the women who shared their lives than that they existed and touched history more or less anonymously; that they lived through periods of the American experience Hawthorne and Melville fictionalized was no doubt part of the appeal these artists had for me. They all formed part of my naked identity in that strip cell: prison officials could not deprive me of them. They helped me to endure.

This work isolates one of the major aspects of the American experience, as analyzed by both Hawthorne and Melville. It argues that at the heart of the American experience is an emptiness. A sense of abandonment. To be abandoned. To abandon. These are the marks of the American identity from the very beginning until now. Out of our abandonment come our acts of violence and our ideologies. Violence is the name for the destruction of that which was abandoned. Ideology is the name for the structure of lies that hides our abandonment.

Both Melville and Hawthorne were responding, I believe, to this aspect of Crevecour as they perceived it in the disparity between his written and his lived words and deeds. They are concerned with cutting through the falsehoods, the myths, the heroes he projected in order to record the truths as they perceived it. Crevecour abandoned his wife and children at the onset of the Revolution and fled to his ancestral home in France. His *Letters* do not reveal that, however; they record his tortured fears for his family's safety, his scheme to join an Indian settlement, his horror of both sides in the dispute, and assorted myths and heroes that belie his and the colonial experience, but, nonetheless, entered into the conceptions Americans and Europeans had about the American identity. Hawthorne and Melville perceived the tragic irony of this great pretender returning to the new republic as a French official only to find his wife dead, his children lost, his farm burned. An alien had indeed discovered, to his great pain, the real American experience.

Abandonment is the original sin of Americans; it is doomed to be repeated endlessly. From the first colonists, who abandoned their homeland, to their children, who abandoned first the old religion, then the old homestead; to all those who, dreading the unknown or poverty, abandoned natives, blacks, and the castaways of their own, white world; to those who abandoned the hedged-in communities for that of the forest; to the New who abandoned the Old Lights; to the Tories who abandoned, or were abandoned by, the Revolutionaries; to every person, cut off by primitive forms of travel, from the hearth and the safety of loved ones—abandonment, to be abandoned, to abandon, these are the signs of our psyche. Hawthorn's *Mosses* and Melville's *Moby-Dick* are classic American works that explore abandonment on every level from the social to the metaphysical.

In our time, Reagan's abandonment of human rights, the poor, blacks, aliens, in favor of military might, vested interest, big business, and holy wars, put forth in rhetoric so reminiscent of the enlightened falsehoods of Crevecour, who discovered new ways of justifying century-old atrocities of arrogance, has led this City on the Hill to 20th century replicas of the Pequot War, and to the brink of utter destruction, which is Melville's prophetic vision in *Moby-Dick*.

* * *

It is sweet to acknowledge my mentors. A volume about each might suffice. Here I can but mention their names. To Dorothy Day, Cesar Chavez, Martin Luther King, Jr. and Ammon Hennacy, I am indebted; for to them do I owe what understanding and sympathy I possess for the "Runaways, Castaways, Solitaries, Gravestones" (as Melville put it) of the American experience. The whaleship can no longer be anyone's Yale College or Harvard, as it was for Melville. My formal education began with the Bowery of the Catholic Worker, the killing fields of migrant workers, and our Federal prisons. I wrote at length about that experience as it happened in *The Catholic Worker* from 1966-1973. Other names occur in those narratives: Smokey Joe, Russian Mike Herniak, Italian Mike, Missouri Marie, Mad Paul, Earl Ovitt, Morry Zatz, Tom F. These, too, are mentors of mine.

A HISTORY OF
ABANDONMENT

JUNE-JULY 1991

"What do you need such heavy rope for?" asked the feedstore owner.

"I need it to tie up my slave," I replied.

"OK," he said, not missing a beat. "I'll show you what we have."

While he measured out thirty feet of inch-think, nylon rope from a large wooden spool amid a nest of other spools, I explained that the rope was meant for Lucky and Pozzo, slave and master from Samuel Beckett's *Waiting for Godot*, that I was directing for our community theater. With black electrical tape he wrapped the thirty foot mark, and then he severed it with a machete. All in a day's work, it seemed. His chore done, he suddenly grew animated as he related his community theater's problems with "Hello, Dolly!"

Hoisting the white coil onto my shoulder, I came away savoring the line, "I need it to tie up my slave," and puzzling over the experience. With its low ceiling and creaky wooden floor, its musty yet lively odor, the feedstore was weirdly apt. I had tried to buy the rope in two state-of-the-art hardware stores nearby, but the self-conscious, somewhat abashed clerks could not provide a rope thick enough.

I needed to say that line in a real setting. I wanted to know how it felt to say it. How the words would tumble from my tongue.

The voice, the tone. The play provided the occasion; the feedstore the site.

For, about the year 1820, Caesar, reportedly one of the first slaves in Wallingford, Connecticut, died at the age of eighty-two years. He was the property of Samuel Cook, whose father and grandfather had, each in succession, owned him since his infancy. In 1755, David Cook, father of Captain Phineas Cook, sold Joseph DeMink, a freeman, born on one of the Cape Verde Islands, into slavery for 52 pounds. His son, the captain, had offered De Mink passage to his homeland, but had bypassed the island and delivered him to his father David in Wallingford. In the 1690s, a namesake of mine, John Cook, most probably an ancestor (things are understandably foggy here) was one of the accusers during the Salem Witch Trials. The earliest Puritan forefather, Henry Cook of Salem, having arrived in 1636, no doubt rejoiced over, if he did not participate in, the Pequot massacre.

Such are some of the burdensome fruits of our family tree before the revolution.

I was only five and could not even count to 150,000; but I remember Hiroshima.

In 1965, amid the body counts from abroad and my students' fractured lives, a colleague of mine in the philosophy department at Hobart and William Smith Colleges took issue with this line from an article I wrote for the college newspaper. ". . . if the war is indeed unjust, those who support it, overtly or covertly, are guilty of murders uncounted of kin, countrymen, and enemy." I left academe in a fit of hubris to teach how to war against war; in the peace movement, at the Catholic Worker. Three years on the Bowery and two more in Federal prison for Refusal of Induction taught me that moral indignation is just a luxury. Nor is it enough to sympathize with "loop'd and window'd raggedness." Audiences do as much. Politicians, too. Doing for them—to feed, clothe and shelter—is necessary, but ultimately that alone will not change the equation. Truly to empathize with humankind, and to stop this unending history of American carnage here and abroad, we must project within ourselves the image, not simply of benevolent master, not simply the hapless victim, but both victim and master. We contain both. It's our heritage. Our bloody inheritance. The experience of being an American teaches us that slave and master share a common root.

Grenada, Panama, and now this utter catastrophe, Iraq, where, within six weeks, we have killed an estimated 100,000 military and no one is counting or even interested in the civilian casualties.

How much triumphant moral guilt can an American bear? Must we commit for every generation the original sins of our fore-fathers? Demonize the other, sanctify oneself; then kill and de-mand others to kill.

"The seventy English [American Puritans] gave the fort a vol-ley of shot, whereat the savages within made a hideous and pitiful cry . . . Pity had hindered further hostile proceedings had not the remembrance of bloodshed, the captive maids, the cruel insolency of those Pequots hardened the hearts of the English [and] in little more than an hour betwixt three and four hundred of them were killed, and of the English only two—one of them by our own muskets . . . The whole work ended, ere the sun was an hour high, the conquerors retreated . . ." (Vincent, *A True Relation*).

General Sherman did not invent total war; the Puritans did. He simply agonized, as leaders of our time have not, over its appli-cation to fellow country people.

Now, total war is waged against a people without even a fort, only sand, to protect them; by a phantom, high-tech army. We are assured by General Powell that there was no intelligence failure. True enough. Intelligence just lied to us. In spite of the smart bombs, the great demon-figure is still in power, while land and dwellings were devastated, leaving 72,000 people homeless; and still no one is interested in the Iraqi dead.

How long can we, in our name, tolerate such abandonment? Can't we change? Have we no shame? Is there really no end to this rope?

IN DEFENSE OF
A GENERATION OF
OBJECTORS

March-April 1997

[The following is a letter by Jack Cook to the editor of Naval History in response to an article entitled "The Vietnam Fault Line" by Robert Timberg that appeared in their August, 1996 issue. The article is the text of an address, largely based on Robert Timberg's book The Nightingale's Song, given at the US Naval Academy in Annapolis, Maryland. In the book, he chronicles the lives of John McCain, Robert McFarlane, Oliver North, John Poindexter and James Webb. All five graduated from the US Naval Academy and were, except for John Poindexter, combatants in the Vietnam War, as well as having important roles during Ronald Reagan's presidency. As Mr. Timberg writes, he wanted to treat the "five as metaphors for the emotions, motivations and beliefs of a legion of well-meaning but ill-starred warriors." Mr. Timberg, himself an Annapolis graduate and veteran of the Vietnam War, identifies a "fault line between those who fought the war and those who used money, wit and connections to avoid battle.

The response printed below was not published by Naval History. Jack Cook was an associate editor of the Catholic Worker in the 1960s and is the author of Rags of Time: A Season in Prison.—Eds. Note.]

Dear Sir:

Permit me to come to the defense of the "unbloodied" half of Mr. Timberg's generation. Those men who, according to him, "used a vast smorgasbord of deferments—often relying on a large network of draft counselors—to beat the system and avoid or evade the draft."

First of all, it was not avoidance or evasion we were teaching at the time. It was principle, conscience and commitment. To kill on command may be duty for a professional soldier, but, to a private citizen it should be unthinkable. Draft counseling was aimed primarily at the men who had not yet taken any oath. The Peace Movement had one objective—to stop the war, but it had two paths to that end: first, to raise the consciousness of the American people by demonstrating , etc.; second, to stop the draft by denying Selective Service the bodies they demanded. We did stop the draft as we know it; the government just created a new machine to reap its fodder, the Lottery. And, by 1968, the American people, sick of the war and the turmoil at home, blindly elected Richard Nixon, peace candidate with his "secret" plan for peace.

It is futile to deny the events and disclosures of the last 30 years, from the Pentagon Papers to Robert McNamara's confessions. I will not argue the war. Suffice it to say that, if the commander and his effort are unjust, then it is not only unthinkable to kill on command, it should be resisted. Those who chose to resist should not be condemned for the manner in which they resisted, whether it be getting married, leaving the country, disrupting their health, or whatever. For physical courage, on the playing field and the battle field, there are awards and medals: but who is out there to judge moral courage? Not I. Not you, I think. I agree with the former prisoner of war, John McCain, as quoted in Mr. Timberg's book, *The Nightingale's Song:* "They [the alleged draft dodgers] have to judge whether they conducted their lives in the best fashion, not me."

Does it take moral courage to follow the accepted role of the draftee and step forward to deliver the expected oath of allegiance? Yes, we answer. And does it take moral courage not to follow the accepted role and not to step forward to deliver the expected oath? Yes, I answer, especially when such an act goes against all one's early training, as in the cases of the sons of military servicemen, or the accepted mores of society, as in the cases of just about everyone else. Both require courage. Who can weigh them? Yet the former can be said to represent the courage to be as I am expected to be, while the latter represents the courage to be as I think I ought to be. To those who saw an unjust war, and participation in it as unjustified killing, that "no" to the oath was, I affirm, as courageous as the informed "yea" of his peer.

Of course there were cynics—those with no beliefs, no values, no truth, no meaning—on both sides. But we are talking millions here: according to Robert Timberg, eleven million who took the oath, sixteen million who did not. Who can draw the percentages? Whatever the number, it is this moment that defines, not the subsequent choice of ways.

If the percentages cannot be calculated, how then can the individual ways to say "no" be evaluated? Should I be grateful to Mr. Timberg and Senator John McCain for giving me the nod, as one who went to prison rather than war? Putting oneself in harm's way, as any soldier knows, may be but hubris, not courage. To marry unprepared? To drug one's system to lifelong debilitation? To leave one's family, friends, career for a foreign land? Are there not perils there? Who is bold enough to judge? Not I. Not you, I think.

I agree with John McCain, again, when he affirmed, as reported by Mr. Timberg, that "the top generals and admirals should have resigned in protest, preferably *en masse*, his father included." But they did not. And the killing went on. So did the resistance. According to Mr. Timberg's book, 60 percent of the 27 million draft-age men "escaped military service by a variety of legal and illegal means." Not escaped; rather resisted. Do what you can, you cannot square the number with the number of graduates of elite colleges and universities. We reached others as well, everywhere. My draft counseling went on mainly on the Bowery, but also wherever in the country I found myself as a speaker and writer for the radical *Catholic Worker*.

While still a young Instructor in English at Hobart and William Smith Colleges, I wrote an article for the college newspaper, in November 1965, about a seminar held on the war; the conclusion, in part, reads:

Finally, in response to Mr. Smith's cryptic remarks about conscientious objectors, to the effect that if they are honest and sincere, the government should suffer a few of them, let me say that I will advocate and support, I will celebrate and applaud a generation of objectors—of objectors with a consciences not atrophied, with moral principles not benighted, with political positions not distorted by vested interest, income or status, with intellectual commitment not grooved or rooted in one or another of the disciplines, and with values superior to their elders . . .

I quit academe with its essential occupation deferment, returned my cards to the draft board and joined the Peace Movement to teach how to war against war. In 1968, I was indicted and convicted for Refusal of Induction and sentenced to three years in Federal Prison.

I want to say, most emphatically today, that I celebrate and applaud that generation of objectors, with the exception of the Gingriches, Lotts, Limbaughs, and Wills, who, as Mr. Timberg rightly observes, "dodged the draft" only to emerge later as "champions of the Reagan administration's tough-talking foreign policy." The "chicken hawks" as he calls them; the "War Wimps" as Jack Newfield and Mike Royko called them.

But that bunch, despite their capacity to abuse their power, do not amount to a hill of beans in relation to those, who, quietly, after the agony of those years, resumed their lives alongside the rest of their generation. For the "fault" that Mr. Timberg describes does not exist, despite his efforts to create it; it is, I fear, but the "undigested lump" of hate he understandably retains for those who did not go to Vietnam. But we all went to Vietnam, and, if words mean anything beyond their literal content, came back bloodied. To project that hate onto a whole generation is to do a great disservice, especially if directed at a new generation. Such factionalism aimed at one's fellow countrymen is fraught with danger. Governments, when they are wrong, should be resisted. That is only patriotic, after all. It is the country and its people that we love, not the arrogance of power to which its leaders, at times, seem devoted.

To address Mr. Timberg's major point: "The problem with Vietnam was the homecoming." To be spat upon and called "baby killer" were loathsome responses. That it happened cannot be denied; that the Peace Movement was responsible cannot be affirmed. The movement consisted of, among older pacifist groups, such new ones as Vietnam Veterans Against War and the GI activists within the military. According to Terry Anderson, in his *The Movement and the Sixties*, in 1971, "some 25,000 personnel took undesirable discharges." And the number of desertions during the war set a record—over half a million soldiers deserted. On what side of the fault line do those soldiers belong? Re-enlistments fell to the lowest on record. At Annapolis, since 1968, four classes had failed to meet their Marine quotas, as Mr. Timberg notes.

The Peace Movement was not doing the spitting, nor were the returning anti-war GIs; for, contrary to Mr. Timberg's assertion in his book, we did make common cause "with our peers in uniform." The only explanation outside of mob psychology is that the response parallels the response of returning GI activists, who, as Mr. Timberg writes, "hurled their medals at the steps of the Capitol." They were responding to the symbols of an unjust war and its leaders, who could not appear without protest in public. The returning soldiers became the maligned surrogates of the president, his advisors, and the military leaders who, as John McCain notes, would not resign.

It saddens me to think of Mr. Timberg's hatred, that undigested lump, that he directs against the movement opposed to the war that he thinks "prevailed." None I know, who so opposed, think they prevailed. We did not stop it. The war went on for fifteen years with too many deaths, too many painful reconstructions.

Yours in peace,
Jack Cook

AN OPEN LETTER TO
THE *CATHOLIC WORKER*

Jane Sammon, Editor
The Catholic Worker
36 East First Street
New York City

Dear Jane Sammon:

When I stated, during my session of the symposium on Thomas Merton and Dorothy Day at Rivier College in April, that Cardinal O'Connor's effort to make Dorothy Day "the patron saint of the Pro-Life Movement," as he is reported to have said, amounted to spiritual abuse, I knew from the sharp applause followed by utter silence that I had touched a nerve as well as insulted a cardinal. I had not time during that session to expand on the notion, and we, in the format of the weekend, had not time to discuss it at length. Hence, this letter.

You were not there when, twenty-five years ago, after seven years as an editor, including two years in federal prison for draft refusal, my name slipped from the masthead of the CW as I pivoted back into private life to restructure and to write.

Although I continued to publish in the Worker isolated pieces over the years, I was not in the city nor involved in the work there, and did not meet you until the symposium, to which I was invited to read from the Prologue of my book, *Rags of Time: A Season in Prison*: a tribute to Dorothy and her anarchist predecessor Emma Goldman.

But before I leap to defend an obviously uncharitable (yet accurate) remark, let me tell you about Sunday morning, the last day of the symposium.

The hotel I was staying in failed to make the wake-up call for 8 am that I requested the night before. I was aware of the time change coming up and mentioned that to the clerk. I was assured the call would be made. But when I did awake, it was already after 9 and I knew I could not make the Liturgy on time. I showered and packed and was at the desk, in an angry mood, for it was useless to complain and I just wanted to leave for home. I did mention to the clerk that the call had not been made, and a young woman standing there echoed my dismay. Then she asked if I was going to Rivier, for she needed a ride there. I did not recognize her from the symposium, but, immediately changing my mind about going home, I said I would drive her. We left for my car and it was in the car that I told her I had had to miss the performance of "Haunted by God"—a one-woman play about a young Dorothy—the night before and now I had to miss the Liturgy. It was then that she said that she was Dorothy. She was Lisa Wagoner, the actress, whose performance I had missed in my anxiety not to spoil a show by having to leave precipitously and perhaps more than once.

Now my love for the theater is as absurd as my love for the church. During the sixties, we at the Worker were always invited to Julian and Judith Beck's performances; and, when the Bread and Puppet group first arrived in Manhattan, they came to us, for they needed a shepherd for a performance in front of St. Pats during Christmas week of 1967, I think. I was enlisted somehow, though I spoke no German, costumed and masked, and joined the little procession, consisting of two kings, St. Joseph, and Mary with a blood-spattered Christ-child. It was piercing theater for all concerned: I was, at one point, by a pedestrian pushed into traffic, and, later, had a dollar bill thrust into my hand.

But none of that really prepared me for sitting suddenly next to a young Dorothy in my Taurus, a real apparition of her anyway, and ad libbing awkwardly lines I did not know from whence they came, while feeling wildly like Didi next to Gogo in a weird update of Godot. I remember remembering in a flash, and telling Lisa about, Dorothy driving me in the old VW beetle to the printers in the Bronx on the days we put the paper to bed. She always drove.

But it is no wonder we got lost on the way to the college, neither of us knowing the area, and I being out of mind, yet arriving at the chapel in time for communion, even though we were so incredibly late and so repeatedly delayed.

For me though it will always be Dorothy who met me at the hotel desk, when I was in an angry and despairing mood; she needed a ride and she kept me from leaving the symposium. So I remain, haunted by Dorothy.

Now, about her canonization. I offer these remarks in the spirit of Peter Maurin's "clarification of thought." I know I have no authority to speak for the Worker; I simply wish, as one who did live and work for D.D. and her ideas, to speak for the workers. I appreciate the delicate situation the Worker is in: it cannot and should not appear to be lobbying for sainthood, for there is potential scandal in such a position. Yet to deny Dorothy sainthood is to deny her her reality. She was a saint—for our (indeed for any-) time—but a very difficult saint. Such was the saint I paid tribute to in that Prologue: no anachronistic spirituality here; rather dogged, enduring nay-saying to injustice, and dogged, enduring yea-saying, in word and deed, to the community of humankind.

The third and best alternative, unfortunately, is unavailable: to let posterity take care of Dorothy and let her, with Mandelstam say:

Yes, I lie in the earth, moving my
lips
But what I shall say, every
schoolchild will learn.

As you know, at the symposium I was put in with the poets, including Dan Berrigan, (whom I had not seen since my wedding in the soup kitchen a week before my imprisonment in 1968), and we were asked what connection did we find between Day and Merton, or something to that effect, and I took the opportunity to say that they met most poignantly for me where they in their own way confronted the church. I like to picture them in my mind, on either side of a blank church wall: Merton, conflicted of course, on the inside yearning to be out; Dorothy, conflicted as well, on the outside yearning to be in. Reified once again, they are mimes, the wall invisible: saints and the universal church.

If the first Pope John Paul had lived to see Dorothy die and had then initiated her canonization, as in my reading of him he would have been inclined to do, I would have supported that effort, for I think he had a real appreciation of D.D. that transcended his Cold War time and place. I'm all but sure that D. herself would not have objected to such an offer from a pope who sent Cardinal Cooke down to the Bowery to bestow his greetings to her. So it is not the fact of canonization I oppose at all. It is the spirit in which, as far as I can judge from what is reported, it is done currently by Cardinal O'Connor that I object to. Dorothy, I'm sure, never anticipated the greeting from Pope John Paul I, and had not that in mind when she used to say she did not wish to be called a saint, did not want to be dismissed that way.

What did she mean by that? Interpretations will vary, of course; but, since the Cardinal has been reported to have said, "Her horror at being called one . . . is itself a saintly attribute," it is necessary to look closely at her words.

Is it horror that Dorothy felt? Horror, perhaps, at being so highly regarded, put into the pantheon, so to speak? Or horror, perhaps, at, as you mentioned, entering that childhood world of the Irish Catholic—"Och, she's a saint sure enough"—and not being entirely comfortable there? It is quite possible D. had the latter response in mind: that she would be quite put off to be dismissed as just a saint in that mode of sentimental piety. But that would require us to believe that her understanding of sainthood stopped there and did not expand to the real saints of consequence, living and dead, that she did live in relation to, for she could not say, in reference to them, that she did not wish to be in their company. (For she was not alone, nor were we then: Martin Luther King, Jr., Cesar Chavez, A.J. Muste, to name a few from this land alone). But Cardinal O'Connor, reportedly, would have us believe so: "Her horror at being called one, etc." He must mean by that that it is saintly humility that sparks the horror.

Well, I disagree. First of all, I see no "horror." I heard no horror in her voice when the subject came up and she would deliver herself of that line. Her statement was matter-of-fact, empirical, and a little angry. What she meant, I think, is that she was more than just a saint, she was at the very least a saint; and here it is not humility, as the Cardinal reads it, but that "hubris of sanctity" that Arthur Koestler writes about, that comes into play: she saw, I think, how they would use her and she was rejecting it beforehand.

To regard her as a saint, in all the fullness of that term, and true though it certainly is, is nonetheless to regard her only partially; it is to disregard her major role as social activist, defender of the poor on more than just religious grounds; to dismiss her distinctly American voice of Christian Anarchism, her place in the American radical tradition, where she holds the unique position as one who, largely in opposition to the church that "scandalized" her, showed that church where its social concerns should be and how, without structure or hierarchy, they might be attained. It is to dismiss her place in the twentieth century political thought, for, and here I disagree with Berrigan and others, her misspent youth was not misspent; it was a glorious youth spent among the best minds of her generation; and from them she learned commitment and solidarity and compassion for the powerless, and to those Communistic and Anarchistic ideals she added, after her conversion, the specifically radical Christian dimension. To write off her "hedonistic" youth is to do her a great disservice. If you dismiss that, you cannot logically account for her conversion, to say nothing of her radical approach to the poor; for, absent her youthful attachments, political, social, and personal, you would have to argue that with conversion came her radical sense of solidarity with the poor. But it is obvious from the record that her concern with the poor predated in vital and substantial ways her conversion, and that her conversion gave her a new and now religious way of confronting the same social and political evils that her generation was facing in secular ways, that she herself had faced in secular ways before her conversion. She may have found those approaches one-dimensional after conversion, but she never dismissed the commitment and sense of sacrifice those approaches generated. She just added another dimension to them and thus transformed Catholic social thought in our time, in the America Catholic church, it is to be hoped.

All this is old news. The new news is, in the effort to canonize Dorothy now in progress, Cardinal O'Connor is on record as saying (USA TODAY, March 12, 1998) Day could become "the patron saint of the pro-life movement."

Now I'm certain there are men and women in that movement who are in all good conscience devoted to their goals. But those goals, I would argue, are not in their political manifestations anywhere near what Dorothy believed in and worked for. In her long pilgrimage, she never made abortion into a political issue; she could not conceive of the notion that poor women's sexuality is the cause of poverty; she would have been outraged that her very term "Personal Responsibility" was usurped to name the new welfare reform bill that only creates longer souplines and greater pain. The whole idea of Dorothy in favor of a legal and political response to abortion is foreign to her. When she spoke of abortion, it was in terms of forgiveness, not criminality.

She could have, at any time, come out publicly and politically against abortion. It would have been gleefully accepted by the church. She did not. She did not overtly support anti-abortion advocates, nor did she approach politically the other issues connected with pro-life: anti-homosexuality and anti-feminists, in or out of the church. To think she would runs counter to her position with regard to freedom of the individual and freedom of conscience.

I must conclude that, for her, these were issues of conscience. Personal issues. Family issues. The church's role, in this perspective, is to forgive when necessary and support always. It is not, I think, the church's role to lobby with the Christian Right to force legislation down the throats of all women, mothers, grandmothers, teens, here and abroad. That runs so counter to D.'s stance that I cannot even contemplate it.

But that is what O'Connor's position forces us to contemplate. It is that misuse of Dorothy, that appropriation of her being, that (to use your word) "revisionist" approach, that makes me speak out on this issue.

Some would, of course, argue that D. was an extremely orthodox Catholic, and therefore likely to support the church here, and they would cite her rosary, her masses, etc. While all that and more is true, and consistent with the behavior of other converts to Catholicism, it is just as true to say that she saw very clearly when the church was simply human, fallible, and nationalistic. Her last speech in public was directed against the church celebrating a mass in honor of Catholics in the military—on Hiroshima Day! They were misusing the Mass and she called them on it.

During the Viet Nam war, in which Cardinal O'Connor served as a chaplain, Dorothy lost editors one after the other to prison for conscience' sake; we, along with the Amish, Mennonites, JW's, Quakers, Black Muslims, Civil Rights and Leftist activists, and solitary, apolitical beautiful souls, served our time as prisoners of war (although not acknowledged as such by the government), and Dorothy supported all of us with her prayers and her paper. And if some while inside, under the strain, broke and lost for a time principles and faith (as did some POWs in Hanoi Hilton), cracked, compromised, adopted the rhetoric of our captors, that is our countrymen, the violence-crazed products of the American capitalist empire, who is out there to judge them but themselves, as Sen. John McCain, a POW himself, has said? Had we followed the church's lead at that time, we would have been over there killing on command and with the church's blessing . . .

Finally, I must respond to the old chestnut of orthodoxy: that statement of hers about shutting down the work if a bishop told her to. We know, at the time of her conversion, she was reading William James' *Varieties of Religious Experience* and would have read the story of St.Ignacius: had the pope told Ignacius to embark on a ship without sail, mast, or rudder, he would do so out of obedience. That is what saints do; they obey higher authority even when it is absurd. Sublime Folly. Dorothy's statement, I think, echoes Ignacius'. But what is not being said by such obedience is that the church is right and therefore I obey. It is the contrary. The church is wrong and its error made manifest by my obedience. Had the church ordered Dorothy to stop she would have, as she threatened, done so—with her workers at St.Pats in a public display of absurd obedience. For all the world to see. The church knew it could not order her to stop without looking ridiculous. That obedience of Dorothy's was orthodox—that is consistent with the behavior of saints—but it was also a radical, not conservative, religious and political statement, which her friends on the left never fully appreciated, for they never knew where she was coming from; and her would be admirers on the right simply refuse to understand out of sheer uncritical devotion to the church.

The painful vision of St.Dorothy, Patron Saint of Pro-Life, comes complete with a de-fanged newspaper, muted criticism, complicity with a reactionary and exclusive agenda, and further fractures of the Left (our common good!).

I fear they—the church—will misuse Dorothy, even as the state already has, and they should be called on it, even as she did when they dared to misuse the Mass on Hiroshima Day.

Pax,

Jack Cook

"A WOMAN WHO SINNED SO GRAVELY"

from Cardinal O'Connor's letter on his web page
"Dorothy Day's Sainthood Cause Begins" 17 March, 2000

I cannot forgive.
No, I cannot forgive
This hollow halo.
I refuse to forgive.

Though this man is dying.
Dying, he is dying.
Dare mount an offense?
I cannot forgive.

"The wrong kind of pity," wrote O'Neill.
No, I cannot forgive.
Good soldier soldiers on.
I refuse to forgive.

No, I cannot forgive—
How long has the hierarchy
Wanted to say that?
No, I refuse to forgive.

He who blessed our Innocents
To kill and be killed on command,
Dares to say it.
No, I cannot forgive.

No, I cannot forgive.
A plaster Irish saint
Out of holy outrage made.
No, I cannot forgive.

Sin is not sin without intent.
May men who sign the page
On women's woes yet live
To see their own festooned.

I cannot forgive
A deceitful political agenda,
A wholly specious homily.
I refuse to forgive.

Dorothy, playfully filling her bowl
With chunks of black bread, said,
"Who made this soup?"

St. Patrick's Day, 2000